STANDARD GRADE HISTORY

Changing Life in Scotland and Britain

1750-1850

Craig Madden

Hodder & Stoughton
LONDON SYDNEY AUCKLAND

Acknowledgements

The publishers would like to thank the following for permission to reproduce copyright illustrations:
Reproduced by permission of The National Gallery of Scotland, 7th Earl of Mar & Family by David Allan p5 bottom; The Repentance Stool by David Allan p66; A Schule Skailin' by George Harvey p69. The National Library of Scotland p5 top; p14 top; p17; p35; p25 bottom. Scottish Ethnological Archive, National Museums of Scotland p6 top; p14 bottom. Auchindrain, Argyll p7 left. The Mitchell Library, Glasgow District Libraries p7 right; p10; p72. The Mansell Collection p8; p21 top, middle, bottom; p34; p37; p44 top; p46 left; p51; p54 top; p55; p57; p58; p60; p63 top; p65; p71. Reproduced by permission of Punch p11 top; p47; p50; p64; p76 top; p77 top. Aberdeen City Arts Department – Libraries p11 bottom. By Courtesy of the Hopetoun Papers Trust p15 left. Mary Evans Picture Library p15 right; p30; p32 top right; p36; p44 bottom; p77 bottom. Nottinghamshire County Library Service p25 top. The Hulton-Deutsch Collection/Hulton Picture Company p26; p54 bottom; p74 bottom. Aerofilms p32 left. Ann Ronan Picture Library p32 bottom right. The National Trust for Scotland p33. New Lanark Conservation Trust p39 both; p40. By Courtesy of Edinburgh City Libraries p46 right. Sunderland Museum & Art Gallery (Tyne & Wear Museums) p49. The Illustrated London News Picture Library p52. Department of History and Applied Art, National Museums of Scotland p53. Hawick Museum p63 bottom. Country Life p73. Alloway Publishing p74 top. The Annan Collection p76 bottom.

Also in the series:
Scotland and Britain 1830-1980 ISBN 0 340 542128
SAS Chalmers and Larry Cheyne

Co-operation and Conflict: International Relations 1890-1930
ISBN 0 340 54214 4
JA Harkness, H McMillan and D Moore

International Relations 1930-60 ISBN 0 340 54211 X
Robert Doig

People and Power: Germany 1918-39 ISBN 0 340 54213 6
Ian Matheson

British Library Cataloguing in Publication Data
Madden, Craig
Scotland and Britain: 1750-1850.
– (Standard grade history)
I. Title II. Series
941.07

ISBN 0-340-53282-3

First published 1992

Typeset by Litho Link Limited, Welshpool, Powys, Wales.
Printed in Great Britain for the educational publishing division of Hodder & Stoughton Ltd, Mill Road, Dunton Green, Sevenoaks, Kent by Thomson Litho, East Kilbride.

CONTENTS

SERIES PREFACE

The books in this series are designed to present major historical themes, change, co-operation and conflict, people and power. Key ideas in British, European and World history derived from these themes provide the basis for the organisation of content. The books make use of different types of evidence – primary and secondary, written, statistical and pictorial. Users of the books are guided towards their own understanding of history, based on their individual abilities and interests, as each section (chapter) progresses from simpler statements of ideas and issues to a consideration and analysis of more detailed and complex evidence.

It is the hope of the authors that the books in the series will increase understanding of the chosen themes as well as enthusiasm for investigating people, actions and events in history. Those who use the books will be encouraged to decide for themselves about the evidence they contain and to have their own views of the past.

Graeme Coy.

SCOTLAND 1750

Scotland in 1750 had a small population, little good land for farming and was still trying to adjust to the union with England in 1707.

It was not a wealthy country, though a few people did enjoy a very comfortable life. Look at the picture of the Earl of Mar and his family. You can see clearly the evidence of his prosperity and importance.

Compare the surroundings of this rich member of the aristocracy with those of the weaver's family from Islay.

During the 100 years following 1750 life changed greatly for most people in Scotland and the rest of Britain. For some the changes brought success and riches: for many life did change but not always for the better.

In the pages which follow you will find information and evidence about the years between 1750 and 1850. Some will be in what people who lived then wrote or drew. Some will be in reports, records and charts made then or later. You can use the evidence to decide for yourself how much life had changed and improved for the people of Britain by the middle of the nineteenth century.

Islay family illustration

Mar family illustration

1 POPULATION

People on the move

The population of Britain began to grow rapidly between 1750 and 1850. This can be seen in the graph below.

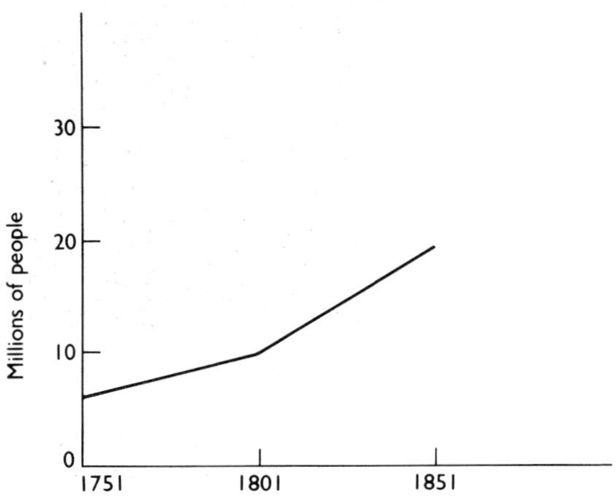

Population of Britain 1751-1851

The rise in the population meant that there were more people looking for work. It was in towns that most jobs were to be found. Therefore, there started a steady movement of people away from the countryside to the towns.

	People living in the country	People living in the towns
1751	80%	20%
1801	75%	25%
1851	46%	54%

New methods of farming meant that many families lost their land and could no longer find work in the countryside. Old ways of life in villages began to disappear. Many people were forced to leave the land in search of jobs and better wages. Machines like Patrick Bell's reaper did the work of many men.

A Bell's Reaper 1831

B The old flax mills, which formerly gave employment to numbers, now employ very few.

New Statistical Account, Inverkeilor (Angus), 1845

C Population has lately decreased in the country part of the parish by the union of small farms. About 40 years ago there were 16 farms in the barony of Fullford; there are only 8 at present . . .

Old Statistical Account, Parish of Houston and Killallan, 1794

D The decrease is solely the result of throwing a number of farms into one for sheep grazing, and setting adrift the small tenants.

New Statistical Account, Bracadale (Skye), 1845

?

1. Make 3 pie charts to show the percentage of the population living in the towns, and in the countryside in the years 1751, 1801 and 1851.
2. Write down three reasons people left the countryside according to the sources.

GROWTH OF TOWNS

From around 1750 thousands of families began to flood into towns and cities of Britain. As a result, cities like Manchester, Liverpool and Glasgow grew very rapidly over the next 100 years.

Let us follow the story of the McDougal family who lived in a small croft in Lochgoilhead in Argyllshire.

E McDougal family croft

Their minister Mr Dugal McDougal tells us why they had to leave.

F The great decrease in the population of the parish was owing to the introduction of sheep. Most of those who were dispossessed of their farms settled in the towns on the Clyde.

Sir John Sinclair, An account of the Systems of Husbandry adopted in the more improved Districts of Scotland, *1814.*

The McDougal family made the long journey south by foot. They found work in the Coatbridge Iron Works. This is what their new home was like.

G It is anything but beautiful. Dense clouds of smoke roll over it all the time. Flakes of soot fill the air, and settle on your face.

Report of the Commissioners on the Employment of Children, 1842.

H McDougals' new home

Other evidence shows us how families on the move caused the growth of different towns, such as Lochwinnoch, Airdrie and Dundee.

I The population has increased rapidly since 1791. The chief reason was the building of cotton mills about that time.

New Statistical Account, Lochwinnoch, 1845

The increase in population is owing to the coal works in the parish.

New Statistical Account, Airdrie, 1835

The cause of the extraordinary increase in population since 1821 is due to the great growth in the linen trade.

New Statistical Account, Dundee, 1845

?

1 Match up the towns with the correct industries that attracted families to move there.

DUNDEE	COAL
LOCHWINNOCH	LINEN
COATBRIDGE	COTTON
AIRDRIE	IRON

2 Describe in your own words what happened to the McDougal family. The following points should be in your account:
- How they felt about leaving their croft.
- What did they think about Coatbridge?
- The differences between Argyll and Coatbridge.

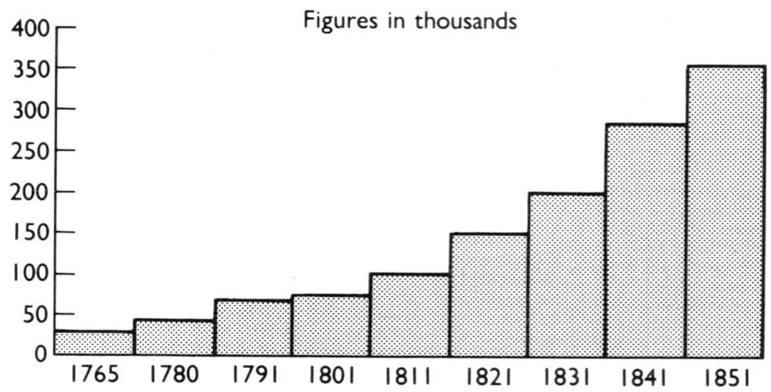

The Population of Glasgow

THE POPULATION GROWS AND GROWS

The population of Britain grew rapidly in the 100 years after 1750. In Scotland it rose from around 1.25 million in 1750 to 2.90 million in 1851. Most of this increase was in towns, like Glasgow.

There were similar increases in English cities. In Birmingham the population rose from 70,000 in 1801 to 200,000 in 1851, while at the same time Manchester rose from 75,000 to 225,000.

It is difficult to know how accurate these figures are. For the eighteenth century, we have to rely on estimates. In 1755 the Revd Alexander Webster, an Edinburgh minister, estimated the population of Scotland by relying on information provided by his fellow ministers from their parish records. Such evidence could be inaccurate and misleading, although his final figures were probably not too inexact. The first census was in 1801, and continued to be taken every 10 years. Although the early census asked very simple questions, it was now possible to show how the population in certain areas was either rising or falling over a 10 year period.

Although we know that the population of Britain was rising, by as much as 15 per cent in some decades, it is more difficult to find the reasons for the increase. Immigration was a possible cause, but figures suggest that as many people left Britain as came in during this period. The other two possibilities are a rise in the birth rate, or a fall in the death rate.

J Taking the census

A healthier population

As a result of agricultural improvements, people in Britain were able to enjoy a better and more varied diet. Bread, potatoes, meat, milk, cheese, fruit and vegetables were now readily available for most of the population. Despite this it was the poor who were to suffer the most during famines or when the potato crop failed in the 1840s.

Medical treatment also improved at this time. More hospitals were built, but they were still only scattered throughout the country. The chances of infection in these hospitals was very high, and may have increased the number of deaths among the sick.

Most medical improvements did not occur until after 1850, except for the introduction of vaccination by Edward Jenner in 1796. It proved to be an effective method of preventing the spread of smallpox; in London the death rate from the disease fell from around 800 in every 10,000 in 1750 to only 100 by the mid-nineteenth century. Epidemic diseases like bubonic plague had died out by this time, but were replaced by other diseases like tuberculosis and cholera, the latter killing over 50,000 in 1831. There was, however, an improvement in the number of children who survived their first five years.

K Children who died in London before the age of five

1730-1749	=	75%
1750-1769	=	63%
1770-1789	=	52%
1790-1809	=	42%
1810-1830	=	32%

Estimates from Dr Andrew Combe, 1840

Better housing

By 1850 better housing conditions were to be found in some parts of Britain's cities. Better quality houses were built of brick and tiles, piped water and drainage systems were being built, but still the majority of the urban poor lived in appalling poverty in the slums. But, there were big improvements in personal hygiene which must have reduced the spread of disease. With the introduction of cheaper soap and better water supplies, more people were able to wash themselves and their clothes. Cheap cotton cloth meant that people could keep warmer, while more coal resulted in drier and warmer houses.

Bigger families

As industry expanded in the towns, there were many more jobs for the young workers. More reliable employment resulted in people marrying earlier and being better able to afford to feed more children. The effect was to reduce the normal age of marriage from 27 in 1700 to around 20 by 1800. Larger families became more common, and as child labour in the factories increased, the children could be sent out to work at an early age to earn their own keep.

?

1. Why is it difficult to find accurate figures for population changes between 1750 and 1850?
2. Group work.
Each group should make a list of the factors that could affect the birth rate and the death rate. Each group should then prepare a report of their views on changes in the birth rate and the death rate in the 100 years after 1750. Each report should be read to the whole class.

PEOPLE COMING AND GOING

Between 1800 and 1850 many families left their homes in Ireland and the Scottish Highlands. Their reasons were often the same; poverty, no jobs and no money to pay the rent. They hoped to find jobs in the factories, mines and iron works in the Lowlands.

In the 1840s, a disaster hit both Ireland and the Highlands, where the poor relied on the potato for food. A letter from 600 highlanders tells us what happened.

L We have to tell you that our potatoes have almost entirely failed and many of us and our children will suffer severely during the next winter. We are on the edge of starvation.

Clearances in the Highlands

In the Highlands there was another reason why the people were forced to leave their homes. Some landowners decided to replace poor crofters with sheep, as there was more money to be made from the sale of wool from the sheep. This was known as the clearances. The sad story was told in 1819 by the Revd Donald Sage from Sutherland.

M To my poor and defenceless flock the dark hour came. At an early hour Mr. Sellar, along with a large body of constables, arrived to start their work. They gave the men, women and children half an hour to pack up and carry off their furniture, and then set the cottages on fire. The roofs and rafters were lighted into one red blaze.

Revd Donald Sage on Strathnaver Clearances (1819) in Memorabilia Domestica

?

1 Explain in your own words why sources L, M and N describe so well the terrible situation facing the poor in the Highlands.

2 You are the editor of a newspaper. Make up a front page story on the 'Highland Clearances'.

Emigration

When the poor people were forced to leave the Highlands, where did they go to? Many went to the Lowland towns. Others stayed in the Highlands and settled on the coast. There they tried to make a living by fishing and collecting Kelp (seaweed). But many left Scotland altogether.

A total of almost 2.1 million people left Britain and Ireland between 1815 and 1850. Of the 110,000 who left Scotland, most families went to settle in Canada, America and Australia.

O Free emigration to South Australia. First class ships leaving Southampton on fixed days each month. Free passage is given to this healthy colony to farm workers, shepherds, miners and tradesmen of good character. The demand for workers is urgent with high wages to ensure the comfort of every good man and his family.

Advert in The Northampton Herald, *1846*

A REAL "SCOTTISH GRIEVANCE."

DUNCAN.—"Oh! but my mother is frail, and can't be sent out of the country in that ship; will you not let Flora and her ——"
FACTOR.—[sternly] "No, no lad—move on with the old woman; she will not be here in the way of his Lordship's sheep and deer."

N A real Scottish grievance

There they were promised a new and better life. This could include the offer of cheap and rich land, work for all, wealth and even the discovery of gold in California and Australia in 1848.

P It's better abroad

?

1 What is the cartoon (source P) trying to say about people who went to settle abroad?

2 Design a poster advert trying to sell the idea of a new life in either Canada or Australia.

THE CLEARANCES

From 1750 to 1840 the population of the Highlands increased from 195,000 to almost 300,000 (an increase of 53 per cent). The main reason was the cultivation of the potato, which was cheap and easy to grow on the poor land. It provided the poor crofters with a steady food supply for most of the year.

Q Planting potatoes with seaweed as fertiliser

Although the population increased, there was no extra land, and so families had to grow enough food to survive from smaller plots of land. Some effort was made to introduce new, improved farming methods, but this largely failed as the crofts were too small.

Attempts were made to encourage the Highlanders to learn to catch fish, collect kelp, or even make linen and cotton cloth. There was little success and by 1840 most Highland crofters were already in difficulty.

R The amount of population was rapidly increasing, while the means of support for each family was diminishing. Poverty was speedily making in-roads among the people . . . the causes were the fall in the price of cattle, the failure of the herring fisheries, the cessation of kelp manufacture, and the want of employment.

New Statistical Account, Kilmuir, Isle of Skye, 1840

For many crofting families, the final blow came with the failure of the potato crop in 1846 and again in 1847. They had to leave their homes to avoid starvation. But already many Highland families were being forcibly evicted from their crofts to make way for sheep. Here is what happened in Strathnaver in the County of Sutherland.

Case study: Strathnaver Clearances, 1814

In 1813 the landowner, Elizabeth Countess of Sutherland, decided that more money could be made from leasing her estates out in sheep farms. The rent figures from the Sutherland estates confirm this; in 1803 rents from the crofters amounted to £5,000 a year, but with the conversion to large-scale sheep farms, the annual rent rose to £20,000 by 1820.

Here is what happened at Rhiloisk in Strathnaver.

December 1813	A large sheep farm was set up at Rhiloisk, and Patrick Sellar became the tenant as he offered a higher rent than his competitors. Sellar had said that most of the crofters should leave their homes in Rhiloisk in May 1814. He had a legal warrant to support the eviction of the crofters who had no right to their homes in law.
June 1814	The crofters had not moved, and Sellar began to turn them out and pull down their houses so they could not return. There was a lot of bitterness as most of the crofters had lived there for generations.
July 1814	Although most of the crofters had left by now, they made complaints to the Countess that Sellar had burnt the pasture for their cattle, pulled down their houses, barns and mills before he should have, and carried off their wood which they would use to build new houses.
May 1815	Sellar accused of more serious crimes. As a result he was arrested and sent to prison in Dornoch.
April 1816	Sellar stood trial charged with setting fire to houses in Rhiloisk and the death of three crofters.

R A contemporary illustration of the Highland Clearances

S The deserted townships

T I was present at the pulling down and burning of the house of William Chisholm, in which was lying his wife's mother, an old bed ridden woman of near 100 years of age. When Mr Sellar arrived I told him of the poor old women being in a condition unfit for removal. He replied, 'Damn her, the old witch, she has lived too long: let her burn.' Fire was immediately set to the house, and the blankets in which she was carried were in flames before she could be got out. She was placed in a little shed; she died within five days. Many other deaths resulted from alarm, fatigue and cold; the people being instantly deprived of shelter and left to the mercy of the weather. To these scenes I was an eyewitness.

An account of what happened by Donald Macleod, a stonemason from Strathnaver, in Gloomy Memories.

Many people thought Sellar guilty, but he denied that he evicted anybody who was sick and said that when he set fire to Chisholm's house it was empty. His trial at Inverness lasted 13 hours in a single day and the verdict was 'not guilty'.

What then happened to the evicted crofters? According to Sellar, they left a life of poverty and filth in their former crofts to a more prosperous life in the new fishing villages on the coast. In contrast, the Minister of Tongue said that they had been driven from the peace and plenty of their crofts to hamlets near the shore, where the land 'was now divided among many, and was totally inadequate for all the people to live'.

?

1 Pair work
In pairs, you should write the script to an interview involving a radio commentator and Patrick Sellar. The interview should include around six or seven questions about Patrick Sellar, his involvement in the Rhiloisk clearances, and his trial. The final taped interview should be played to the entire class.

2 The Clearances – right or wrong? Write a short speech on behalf of the Countess of Sutherland in favour of the Clearances, and one on behalf of a crofter from Rhiloisk against them. Who do you think was right?

2 AGRICULTURE

● *The old ways*

In 1750 the methods of farming were inefficient and old-fashioned. Most people lived in small groups of houses known as a ferm toun. The farmers shared the surrounding land, which was made up mostly of bare hillsides, rough moorland and marshland. The land was divided into the infield and outfield. The outfield was often hilly land, sometimes ploughed for poor quality oats, but mostly for grazing cattle.

A The infield, after two or three crops of oats, received all the dung produced from the farm; and then was sowed with barley. It then remained a year as grass; and was ploughed the following season for the same rotation.

William Fullarton, General View of the Agriculture of the County of Ayr, *1793*

The infield was divided into strips of land or rigs. Each farmer had several rigs scattered around the infield. The rigs were often built up to a height of three feet to avoid getting the soil and weeds from the next rig.

Other sources show how primitive the farming system was in 1750.

C The leases were short; and when a farmer has possession for only a few years, he was not encouraged to improve his farm.

Sir John Sinclair, An Analysis of the Statistical Account, *1825*

D Threshing with a flail

This type of farming led to very poor crops. Also the cattle were very thin, and frequently had to be killed before winter because of a shortage of feed. As a result starvation often came to the ferm touns.

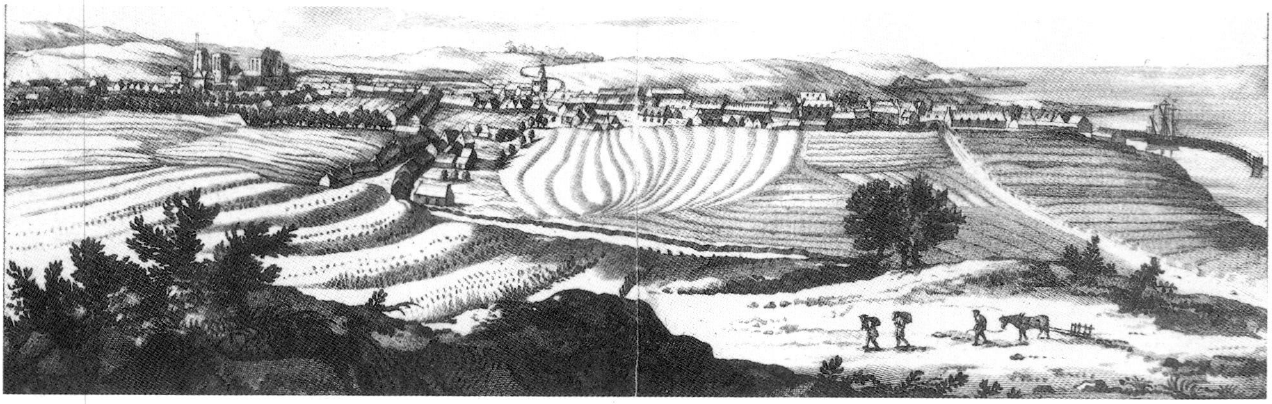

B Rigs near Abroath

Improvements

During the eighteenth century, many Scottish landowners made regular visits to England. There they saw new farming methods at work. As a result, many landowners started to introduce these improvements to their farms in Scotland.

The rigs in the open fields were to be enclosed into compact fields. These new fields were surrounded by either trees, hedges or dykes. At the same time, the marshy land was drained and ploughed for crops.

E The enclosed field

Lime, cow dung and even seaweed were used to manure the land to obtain better quality crops. But, there were many other ways that both landowners and farmers could improve their land and crops.

F The farms in this parish are half in crops and half in grass and clover. The first crop is oats; the second, barley; the third, oats; the fourth, turnips, potatoes, cabbage and peas; and the fifth year barley and grass seeds.

Old Statistical Account, Parish of Careston, Angus, 1792

Leases were usually for 19 years but 31-year leases were not uncommon.

G A threshing machine

The result was a large improvement in the crop yield by 1820. Also, quality of livestock improved. Turnips as winter feed increased the size of the herds, while famous cattle breeds like Aberdeen Angus for beef and Ayrshire for dairy products were developed.

?

1. There are some words about farming mixed up in a list below. Place the ones which refer to *farming in 1750* in one list, and the ones which refer to *farming in 1820* in another list.
   19 year leases : runrig : outfield : Ayrshire cows : turnips : enclosed field : drained land : flail : short leases : threshing machine : marshland : infield : thin cattle : lime.
2. You are going to compare an old farm of 1750 with an improved farm of 1820. These will be your headings for a table. Under each heading you are to write a brief description using the text and sources for the following subjects: the land, manure, crops, leases, threshing, cattle.

THE IMPROVERS

Improvements in agriculture in Britain between 1750 and 1850 were often the result of developments away from the countryside.

1. **Growth of population** – which made the demand for food treble by 1850.
2. **Growth of towns** – where the industrial worker depended totally on the farmer for food.
3. **Improvements in transport** – which made it easier to carry food from the countryside to the town.
4. **Attitude of landowners** – many of whom wanted to make large profits from their lands.

H A Seed Drill and Harrow

Support for farming improvements came from the landowners and the wealthier tenant farmers. The best method was to secure the agreement of all those who held the land. If there was resistance from most of the farmers, then enclosure could be forced through by an Act of Parliament. Such Acts were expensive in legal fees, and to these could be added the cost of new roads, farm buildings, hedges and walls, land drainage, fertilisers and the other essential requirements of farm improvements.

The case of Lord Kames shows both the types of improvements he tried to introduce as well as the attitude of his tenant farmers. Lord Kames obtained the Blair Drummond estate in Perthshire in 1776, and found that 1,500 acres of it was made up of a peat bog, the system of farming was very backward and it lacked roads.

I That country was a miserable sight to an improver; no sown grasses: no turnip for winter feed; the ground everywhere overrun with weeds; and the tenants as poor and indolent. Lord Kames, to instil some spirit into his tenants, begun with promising money rewards for every improvement suited to their capacity. But soon he found his error: so listless were they as to be unwilling to compete for the reward. They had been long in use to pay money to their landlord; but they did not clearly understand what right they could have to receive money from him. The only remedy he had was, to raise their rents; telling them at the same time that if they followed his directions, they would be able to pay their rents better than before; otherwise they must become beggars.

For their encouragement, he distributed among the most deserving tenants the new chain ploughs, for which only two horses are sufficient. Crops of turnips and potatoes in drills are creeping in . . . Lord Kames has engaged to his tenants to enclose every one of their farms, to remove every stone on their land, and to perform every expensive work above their own strength, at a moderate rate of five per cent for the money laid out.

J. Wight, State of Husbandry in Scotland, *1776*

Lord Kames took on the even more ambitious project of clearing the 12 feet of peat and heather from Blair Drummond Moss. The land was leased out in enclosed sections to tenants, mostly from the Highlands. The tenants cut a channel in the moss from North to South, and a mill stream was diverted into the channel. The level and force of the water in the channel was increased by using a large water wheel. The farmers then cut the moss into sods which were thrown into the water channel to float down to the River Forth. The new land then exposed was exceptionally fertile and allowed the farmers to grow fine quality crops. As an encouragement to the farmer, Kames offered a 38-year lease, with the first seven years rent free along with free meal and timber for houses, with the rent rising to 12 shillings (60p) for an acre of cleared land after 19 years and £1.1s (£1.05p) after 38 years. This was clearly a very popular venture; by 1817 a total of 1,130 acres had been cleared of moss, and 186 tenant families now worked their farms on the Moss lands.

Successful landlords, like Lord Kames, were able to charge much increased rents for their lands; for instance, rents in Perthshire rose from 5s (25p) an acre in 1750 to 45s (£2.25p) by 1795. The wealthier tenant farmers who could afford the increased rents of the new improved farms and the costs of the various improvements benefited from the sale of more and better quality grain and livestock at a time of rising food prices. Greater supplies of food also allowed the population to grow, especially in the towns where the flood of factory workers now relied on the improved farms for sufficient good quality food.

However, the improvements did also bring misery and disruption. The poorer tenants who were unable to afford the rents for the new farms were forced to sell out to the richer farmers. Many remained in the countryside and became day labourers on the new farms, frequently living near the poverty line in crowded and rather dismal bothies as a result of low wages and only seasonal work. Many such labourers were later put out of work by the introduction of farming machines, and were reduced to begging. Others left the countryside altogether, and found factory jobs in the towns. The tragedy of the disappearance of the small tenant farmer can be seen in Cadder where 'the parish is now a wilderness . . . the decent families had been reduced to poverty and scattered'.

?

1 Investigation
Find out the name of a landlord as near as possible to your local area who improved his estates between 1750 and 1850. Try and find information which will give you evidence on the following:
the land before these improvements;
the career of the landlord;
the type of improvements introduced;
the effects of these improvements on the people;
the success of the farming improvements.

2 Can you find the evidence which proves Lord Kames was a successful landlord?

3 In all changes there are *winners* and *losers*. Under these headings, write down who you think were the winners and losers during these major changes in farming in Scotland, and give reasons for each of your choices.

*L*IFE ON THE FARM

Changes to the methods of farming brought wealth to the landlords and the tenant farmers. But most people who stayed in the countryside had now become labourers with no land of their own. They worked long hours at back-breaking jobs on the farm.

The best-paid farm workers were called the hinds. Their usual conditions of work were as follows:

- hired by farmers for 6 months or 1 year;
- wages around £14 a year;
- they were given a house tied to the job, and a small plot of land for growing potatoes and vegetables, or for grazing cattle.

Other younger labourers were hired by the farmers day by day only. They were employed normally at Hiring Fairs as reapers at harvest time. Sometimes they had to move around the country to get a job.

Most labourers could only afford the smallest of cottages.

J Cottages at Woodhead Farm

K The house might be 25 ft by 15 ft, in which space is sheltered the hind (labourer) and his family – and in very many cases – the cow and poultry.

Samuel Robinson, Reminiscen[illegible]
Wigtonshire

L Inside a labourer's cottage in Dorset, 1846

M A labourer and his family – in all eight persons – are the occupiers of a hovel, in which there is but one bedroom. There is a small opening with no glass in it which serves as a window. The furniture – a rickety table and two or three chairs.

The Illustrated London News, 1846

The standard of living of farm labourers can be seen by looking at what they earned and on what they spent their money. Source N is the annual budget of a day labourer, his wife and their four children who were all under seven years of age.

N Earnings a year

The man earns as a labourer	£14.18s	(£14.90p)
The woman earns by spinning	£ 5.5s	(£ 5.25p)
Total amount for the year	£20.3s	(£20.15p)
Expenses for a year		
Food – oatmeal, barley meal, milk, onions, potatoes, butter, cheese, bacon meat	£16.14s	(£16.70p)
Clothes for all the family	£ 2.18s	(£ 2.90p)
Loss of time by sickness, bad weather and burials.	£ 0.11s	(£ 0.55p)
Total amount for the year	£20.3s	(£20.15p)

Rent of the house and garden = £1. But the cabbages, greens and potatoes grown in the garden pays for the rent.

Old Statistical Account, Caputh, 1793

The wives of labourers also worked very hard. They had to make the meals, clean the house, look after the children, make and mend the clothes, and tend the cattle and hens. Many were also forced to take on spinning as a part-time job in the evenings. The family meals were often the same every day. The main diet was oatmeal which was eaten in various ways three times a day, and seven days a week. Potatoes and vegetables were added to the meals, and milk, eggs and cheese were also eaten frequently.

?

1 Group display
Each group of pupils is to make up a class display on the issue; 'Life was hard for the farm labourer in the 1790s'. Each member of the group should use one of these headings:

- housing;
- conditions of work for men;
- conditions of work for women;
- cost of living.

Each group should make use of local sources, and other books, to find more information.

The tenant farmer

Improvements in farming greatly changed country life. Ambitious tenant farmers were bold enough to accept the leases of large farms, and then start on a dramatic programme of improvements. Although some such farmers went bankrupt quite quickly others, like Robert Wight on the estate of the great Lothian improver John Cockburn of Ormiston, were very successful.

O Robert Wight, on a farm of several hundred acres, gave an example to the rest. He enclosed his whole farm with hedge and ditch, and planted trees, all at his own expense. He was perhaps the first tenant in Scotland who ventured on so bold an undertaking. Robert Wight was rewarded for his industry. He got a lease from Mr Cockburn of nineteen years, renewable for ever.

A. Wight, The Present State of Husbandry in Scotland, 1778–84

As a result, new-style farmers like Robert Wight were no longer content with the hovels which earlier farmers had shared with their livestock. Instead, the profits of their labours allowed them to build large stone farmhouses with several byres for their increasing herds.

P An improved farm

The profits from the sale of a variety of good quality crops were substantial, as shown by the accounts kept by John Johnstone, a tenant farmer in Berwickshire.

Q

1812	Crops sold			1813	Crops sold		
Wheat	£211	2s	0d	Wheat	£432	10s	9d
Beans	£ 73	9s	0d	Beans	£ 20	13s	6d
Barley	£ 45	17s	0d	Barley	£129	18s	0d
Oats	£ 70	2s	0d	Oats	£ 65	0s	6d
Hay	£106	5s	5d	Hay	£ 20	14s	2d

Accounts kept by John Johnstone, farmer, Dykegateshead, Berwickshire, 1812–13

The day labourer

Although the day labourer was no longer an owner of land, but simply a wage earner, he did not live in great hardship. However, the labourer's life was very insecure; if he lost his job, fell ill or was simply too old to work any more, he would be forced to apply to the parish for poor relief.

Here is the detailed budget of a day labourer in the parish of Auchterarder, who had to support a wife and seven children. He lived in a rented cottage along with an acre of land.

R Income

The father of the family has 1s a day of wages for 8 months, and 10d for the remaining 4 months Deducting 73 days in the year for Sundays, holidays and bad weather, he gains during the whole year	£13	17	0
The mother, with the assistance of the eldest girl, earns by spinning 1s 6d a week, which is a year	£ 3	18	0
The eldest boy earned by tending cattle		18	0
The acre of land produced last year oats, barley, potatoes. Also he sold a calf.	£ 5	9	3
Total	£24	2	3

Expenses	£	s	d
Rent of his house and land	£ 3	0	0
Expenses of cattle feed and management	£ 1	5	0
Fuel	£ 1	5	0
Purchase of oatmeal and barleymeal	£ 8	0	8
The father's wear of clothes; 2 shirts, 2 pair shoes, 2 pair stockings, bonnet and handkerchiefs	£ 1	12	6
The mother's wear of clothes		15	9
Clothes for the children	£ 2	9	0
Soap, salt and candles		10	2
Butcher meat		18	0
Other foodstuffs; cheese, molasses for ale, whiskey, small beer, potatoes etc	£ 2	2	3
Expenses at lying in and sickness		15	10
Grass and straw for the cattle		16	0
Total	£24	0	2

Old Statistical Account, Parish of Auchterarder, 1792

Life for the single labourers was more difficult. They were forced to work long hours in the fields and live in very cramped conditions.

S About four of them are put into a shed, quite far away from the farm house, which shed is called a 'boothie'. Here these men live and sleep, having a certain allowance of oat, barley and pea meal, upon which they live, mixing it with water, or with milk when they are allowed the use of a cow. They are allowed some money besides to buy clothes with. They hire for the year, under very severe punishment in case of misbehaviour or quitting service: and they cannot have fresh service without a character reference from the last master and also the parish minister.

William Cobbett, A Tour of Scotland, *1833*

?

1 Pair work
Each pair of pupils is to make up a questionnaire on the five main features of the lifestyle of the tenant farmer, and also of the day labourer. Your 10 point questionnaire should then be exchanged with another pair of pupils, who will then answer your questions by using sources O to S. Both pairs then compare their answers.

2 Source evaluation
In your study of life in the farming communities after the improvements write a short report on the historical value of sources R and S.

WAR AND TRADE

Britain was at war with France almost constantly between 1793 and 1815. This greatly affected both farming and the lives of people in Britain. The war upset Britain's trade with Europe. Napoleon Bonaparte, Emperor of France, tried to win the war by stopping all supplies of European corn reaching Britain.

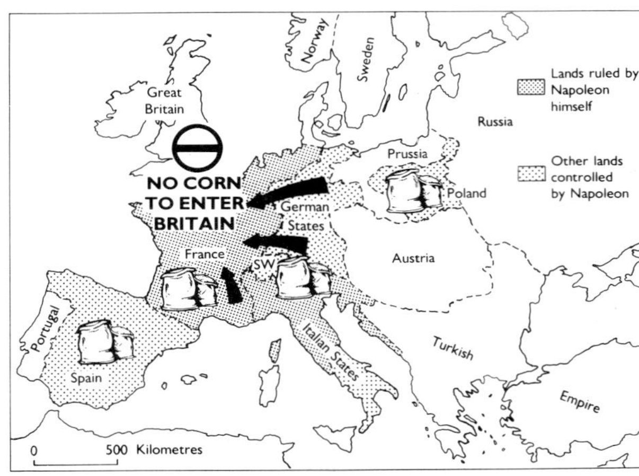

The supply of food in Britain fell during the war years. But there was also a growing demand for food as the population of Britain rose from 8.5 million to 12.5 million during the French wars. As a result, the price of food rose steeply.

T The price of wheat

1789 = 44 shillings per quarter
1794 = 49 shillings per quarter
1799 = 65 shillings per quarter
1804 = 84 shillings per quarter
1809 = 84 shiilings per quarter
1814 = 102 shillings per quarter

BR Mitchell and P Deane, Abstract of Annual Historical Statistics

The high price of food affected people in different ways. Look now at the interviews with a farmer and a farm labourer in 1814. They were both asked the question: – How has the war changed your life?

Farmer

'I have been able to increase my wheat crop by over 40 per cent over the last 30 years. And the high wheat prices have brought me greater profits. But I now have to pay a much higher rent to my landlord. The war has made me much better off.'

Labourer

'My wages have only risen slightly since the war started. But the price of bread has gone up much faster. The result is that I can hardly afford to buy enough bread to feed my family. However, the war has at least made sure that I have a job on the farm ever day.'

U Unable to afford bread, forced to beg

Riot against Corn Laws, breaks up farming machines

Punished for riot

The corn laws

The war against France ended in 1815, and cheap corn from Europe could now come into Britain. This should have been good news for the poor as it would have brought down the price of bread. But this did not happen. To find out why not, let us hear again from the Farmer.

'I am very worried if the price of corn falls. I will not make enough profit to pay my rent, labourers' wages or work my machines. The farm will go out of business. My family could be left in poverty. My landlord is a Member of Parliament, and he says the Government will help me.'

The Government did help the farmers by passing the Corn Laws. These Laws said that no foreign corn would be taken into Britain unless the price of British corn became very high (at least £4 a quarter).

The Corn Laws were very unpopular with the poor in Britain. The price of bread was now being kept high by the Government. Protest riots broke out all over the country. Over 100 shops in Dundee were attacked in these bread riots.

These drawings show what happened to many poor farm labourers as a result of hunger.

?

1. Draw a graph showing what happened to the price of wheat during the years 1789 to 1814.
2. War always changes the lives of ordinary people. Make two lists, one on how people benefited, and the other on how people suffered.
3. Pair work. Firstly, you should decide who is going to be in favour, and who is to be against, the Corn Laws. Then each is to design a poster supporting his or her view.

● *From protection to free trade*

For several hundreds of years the British Government followed a policy of Protection. In order to 'protect' British industry and agriculture, the government placed customs duties or taxes on all foreign imports, making them more expensive than British products. This resulted in higher prices generally, to the benefit of the rich farmers and manufacturers.

However, in 1776 a Scot, Adam Smith, wrote a book called the *Wealth of Nations*, in which he put forward the idea of Free Trade. He believed that Britain would prosper if there was free competition between businesses and between countries, with no hindering duties or taxes. Smith's ideas were so appealing that many British prime ministers, like William Pitt (1783-1801) and Robert Peel (1841-6), introduced new laws based on Free Trade.

But 22 years of war against the French left Britain with many problems in 1815. The Government decided to return to a policy of Protection by introducing Corn Laws, as follows:

> 'foreign corn may be imported into the United Kingdom, for home consumption, without payment of any duty whatever . . . whenever wheat shall be at or above the price of eighty shillings (£4) per quarter.'

This had the effect of keeping the price of wheat at a much higher level than before the war. At a time of rising food prices, the years after 1815 saw much unemployment as a result of more and more machines in factories and on farms, returning soldiers and sailors looking for jobs and the closure of industries making goods for the war. As there was now an enlarged workforce, and growing immigration from Ireland, employers offered lower wages. In Glasgow the average daily wage of a handloom weaver fell from around 2 s 2d (11p) in 1814 to only 10d (5p) in 1819.

The campaign for Free Trade and an end to the Corn Laws started in 1815 and continued until they were abolished in 1846.

V A comment on the new Corn Law of 1815. French traders are offering cheap corn, but the English landlords refuse to allow it in. An angry English worker with his starving family says he will emigrate.

An article in the *Scotsman* newspaper in 1820 put forward the case for an end to the Corn Laws.

W 'Were it not for the Corn Laws, we might be able to purchase bread for 40s or at most 50s, that now costs 70s or 80s. The interest of the farmers is exactly the same as that of the consumer. If prices were permanently reduced, rents would fall in proportion, bad land would be thrown out of cultivation, and the profits from agriculture would rise. By permitting the free importation of foreign corn no real injury would be done to the landlords; for they have no right to benefit at the expense of other classes.'

The Scotsman, 6 May 1820

The campaign against the Corn Laws was stepped up in 1839 with the foundation of the Anti-Corn Law League by two factory owners, Richard Cobden of Manchester and John Bright of Rochdale. The League attracted a lot of money, and from its centre in Manchester it sent out newspaper articles, speakers and pamphlets all over Britain. This poster was used to support the League's cause at an election campaign.

Many Conservative politicians spoke out in favour of Protection, mostly because they believed that the landowners had a traditional right to govern the country, and that their welfare required the high farming profits associated with the Corn Laws. However, the Free Trade case was helped greatly by the failure of the potato crop in Ireland in the late 1840s. Thousands of Irish families starved when a blight destroyed the potato crop which was their main and often only source of food. It was argued that the Irish peasants would be helped if the Corn Laws were repealed and cheap foreign corn could be imported into starving Ireland. As a result, in 1846 the Corn Laws were repealed.

?

1. Evaluation
   Look carefully at sources V, W and X, and in a short report say why you think each source puts forward effectively the case in favour of Free Trade and an end to the Corn Laws.
2. Explain why the campaign to bring an end to the Corn Laws was so successful.

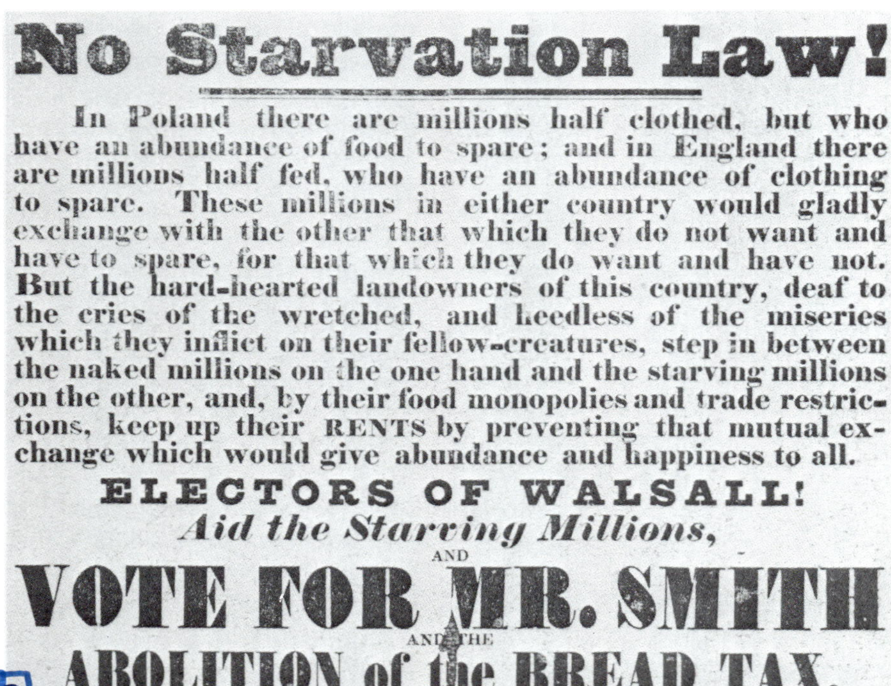

X Anti-Corn Law poster

3 TRANSPORT

The roads improve

Around 1750 the roads in Scotland were little better than stony dirt-tracks. It is not surprising that few people ever travelled more than a few miles from their homes. There were problems in carrying heavy goods like coal, corn or peat more than a few miles.

A The roads were narrow and rough, scarcely passable with carts in the summer and in winter so deep as to hardly passable with horses.

Old Statistical Account, Parish of Cambuslang

B Packhorse Bridge in Yorkshire

Although the Statute Labour Act of 1669 required all local people to work on road repairs for six days in the year, little was done and travel by road remained both slow and dangerous.

C Let me warn all travellers to avoid the road from Preston to Wigan; they are likely to break their necks or their limbs by overthrows or break downs. They will meet here with rutts, which I actually measured four feet deep, and floating with mud from a wet summer. The only mending it receives is the scattering of some loose stones, which do little more than jolt a carriage in a violent manner.

Arthur Young, A Six Months Tour through the North of England, *1771*

The story of Lord Lovat's coach journey from Inverness to Edinburgh shows the problems of road travel.

D I had not gone eight miles when the axle broke in two . . .and I was forced to ride to Ruthven late at night. My coach was pulled there by force of men. A wheelwright and a smith took two days to mend it. I had not gone four miles when it broke again. I was twelve days on my journey, which was seven days more than the ordinary.

From a letter written by Lord Lovat, 1740

Military roads had been built in the Highlands, but they had not been maintained. Travel along the road between Dalmally and Oban was very dangerous.

E The road is so bad as to be scarcely passable for carriages. One is likely to be thrown from a height of four hundred feet into the lake . . . or crushed by rocks which fall from the slopes.

B. Faujas de Saint Fond, A Journey through England and Scotland to the Hebrides, 1784

Improvements in farming and industry created a demand for better roads.
1. Larger farms needed more machines and fertilisers.
2. Growing towns needed greater supplies of food.
3. Factories needed raw materials and coal for fuel.

Turnpike Trusts

Money was collected from local landowners to pay for the improvement of short stretches of road. The money was repaid from tolls collected from the people who used these new roads. These tolls were collected at the Turnpike Gate.

F The Nottingham Turnpike

The road surface

Improvements to the surfaces of roads in Britain was due largely to great roadbuilders like John Metcalf (1717-1810), John Macadam (1756-1836) and Thomas Telford (1757-1834).

Telford's roads had a flat foundation of large stones, a layer of stones no larger than 6cm, and finally a layer of gravel on top.

Telford helped to open up the Highlands by building around 900 miles of good roads and over 1,000 bridges. However, Macadam's roads were often more popular as they were cheaper to build. He used soil as his foundation, on top he put a layer of small stones, and then small stone chips on the surface. He believed that the wheels of carts and coaches would crush the chips into a smooth surface.

H I have made roads three inches higher in the centre than I have at the sides. If the road be smooth, the water will run off easily in such a slope.

J.L. Macadam, Observations on the Highways of the Kingdom, *1811*

The result of these road improvements was to make travel by road quicker, cheaper and safer. Large carts and waggons could safely carry goods long distances. The coach journey between Edinburgh and London was reduced from 10 days in 1750 to 42 hours in 1830.

?

1. Give evidence from sources A to E to show that travel by road in 1750 was both slow and dangerous.
2. Using source G, describe in your own words how Telford went about building his roads.
3. Make a cross-section sketch of Macadam's type of road.

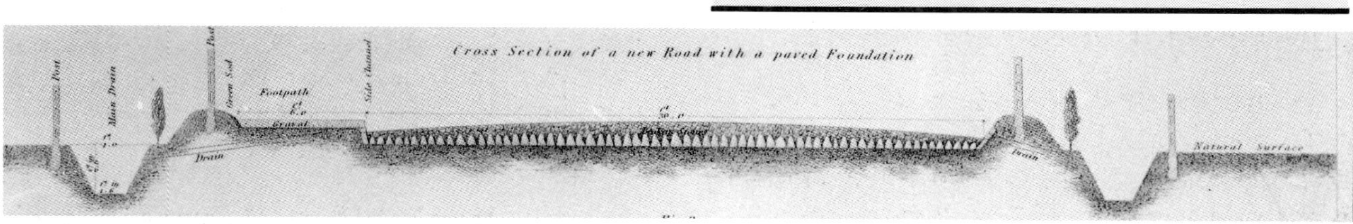

G Telford's Road

THE GROWTH OF TURNPIKE TRUSTS

In the early eighteenth century the first Turnpike Trusts were formed in England to improve the standard of roads. It was not until after 1750 that similar Trusts were set up in the Lowlands of Scotland, either to repair existing roads or to build completely new roads in their place.

An Act of Parliament was required before a Turnpike Trust could be established.

I The roads between Edinburgh and Glasgow, by the deepness of the soil in some places, and their narrowness and ruggedness in other, are in many parts become impassable in winter for wheel carriages and horses, and very dangerous to travellers, and several bridges are in a ruinous condition, a body of trustees, consisting chiefly of landowners, and including the provost and merchants of the city of Glasgow were appointed for keeping the roads in proper order with power to erect turnpikes and levy tolls to meet the expenditure.

Act of Parliament, 1753

However, the cost of such ventures was frequently very high, ranging from £200 to as much as £1,000 per mile in the main roads.

J So that on the whole, the gentlemen of this county (Renfrew), have spent about £100,000 in building a great number of bridges, and in making and repairing above 140 miles of Turnpike Roads . . . a large sum in a small county but necessary in consequence of the great population and extensive manufacturing and commercial establishments in this part of the kingdom.

J Wilson, A General View of Agriculture of Renfrewshire, *1812*

As the Turnpike Trust was regarded as an investment, it was necessary to recover the cost of these new roads from the users. Tolls were charged to travellers at the Turnpike Gates, which were erected across the road to ensure people stopped to pay. People competed for the right to collect the tolls each spring, and the person who offered the most money for the privilege either lived in the tollhouse himself or else paid someone to collect the tolls for him. The law required every tollkeeper to place in front of his house a notice with a list of the toll rates. These rates were based on the type of transport using the road.

K A Mail Coach passes through a Toll Gate

L

County of Edinburgh
Table of Tolls
1809

1. Stage coach, drawn by two horses, carrying passengers:	
Six or less inside, without outside passengers	1s 0d
Six or less inside, with outside passengers	1s 8d
2. Stage coach, drawn by three or more horses, carrying passengers for hire:	
Four inside and two outside passengers	2s 0d
Ten inside and above five outside	9s 0d
3. Every other coach:	
Drawn by 1 horse 6d; Drawn by 4 horses	2s 0d
4. Waggon with more than two wheels	
Drawn by 1 horse 6d; Drawn by 4 horses	4s 0d
5. Loaded carts with two wheels	
Drawn by 1 horse 6d; Drawn by 2 horses or more	8d
6. Saddled horse, with or without rider	2d
7. Every other horse laden or unladen	1½d
8. Oxen or cattle, per twenty	1s 3d

General Turnpike Act, Edinburgh, 1824

The Turnpike Trusts reached their peak around the 1830s, by which time there were over 35,000 km of Turnpike roads in Britain and about 8,000 toll gates. In Scotland alone, there were over 8,000 km of Turnpike roads which linked all the major towns in the country.

But was the Turnpike Trust a success or a failure? Here is a list of comments and statements from different parts of the country which will help to form an opinion.

1. Good quality roads meant that stage coaches could set out daily between Glasgow and Edinburgh, and make the journey between the cities in a day at the cost of 12 shillings for each passenger.
2. An Aberdeenshire minister wrote that the farmers in his parish of Old Meldrum could now get their farm produce to the market in Aberdeen all the year round. As a result these farmers had more money to improve their farms.
3. In 1822 an inspection of the Banff to Fraserburgh Turnpike showed that it had been neglected; the drains were blocked, while there were also a number of large holes in the road itself.
4. In Aberdeenshire a four horse coach could be charged 4 shillings at every tollgate in the county. Passengers were therefore charged high fares to cover the cost of the toll every six miles, and the expense of the coach, horses, driver and guard.
5. In Shotts in Lanarkshire, the public were astonished by the advantages of the new roads; a journey which used to take two days could now be completed in five or six hours, and there was a great increase in the number of packhorses using the roads.
6. The annual revenues from the Turnpike tolls in the Renfrewshire:
   1791-2 = £2,100
   1794-5 = £3,000
   1803-4 = £6,500
   1810-11 = £10,300
7. In an Aberdeenshire parish, the number of carts used for carrying both goods and people rose from 50 in 1790 to more than 300 in 1835.
8. The annual revenue from tolls on the Glasgow to Paisley road are insufficient to cover the very high repair costs, mostly caused by the wet climate, the heavy loads conveyed on the narrow wheels of numerous carts and the 24 stage and mail coaches that operate on this stretch of road.
9. Over 100 miles of new road have been built by the islanders of Skye.

?

1 Which of the sources I, J, K and L has contributed most to your knowledge and understanding of Turnpike Trusts?

2 Make a poster advertising a Turnpike Trust.

3 Debate
Motion:- The Turnpike Trust brought great benefits to the people of Scotland in the early nineteenth century
Groups should discuss the motion, and then prepare a report either supporting or rejecting it. Each report should be read out to the class, and a vote taken at the end.

4 INDUSTRY

From Home to the Factory

During the eighteenth century most of the woollen and linen cloth was made in the home. It was therefore called the cottage or domestic industry. Farming families made their own clothes, but they also made cloth in return for wages. This money was a valuable source of income and helped the family to make ends meet. Cloth making was a part-time industry for the farm labourer's family, usually done in the mornings and evenings or on Sundays. They had no training for this work, the children simply learned the trade from their parents.

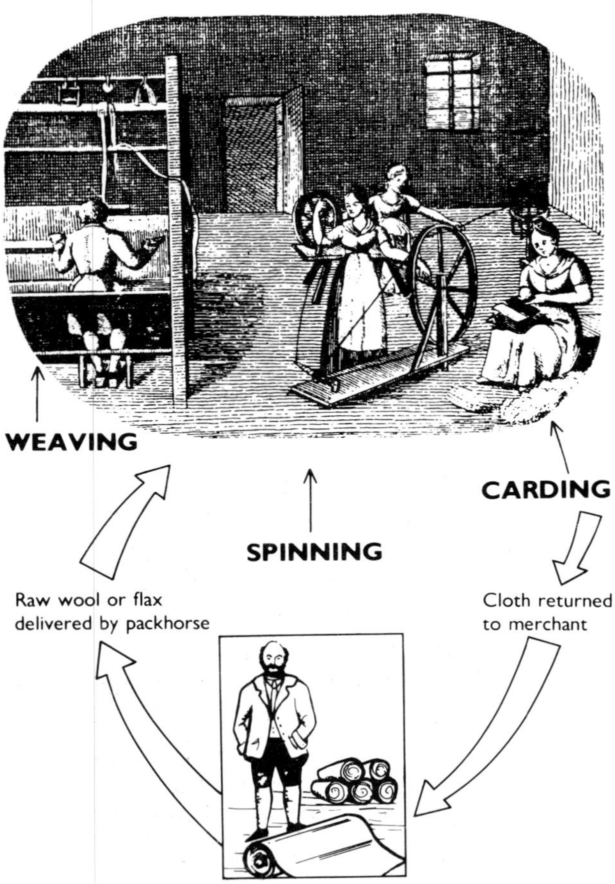

A The Cottage Industry

The process of making cloth from wool or flax was made up of several stages.

1. The wool was washed.
2. The wool was carded by brushing the raw wool into separate fibres with wire brushes. Work done by the daughters.
3. The fibres were spun into thread by a hand operated spinning wheel. Work done by the wife and elder daughters.
4. The thread was woven into cloth by a foot operated loom. Heavy work done by the father.

B Spinning flax yarn on the small wheel and woollen yarn on the large wheel . . . took up the time of every hardworking woman early and late. Throughout my mother's life she was used to rise very early, by five or six o-clock, even in cold winter mornings, to spin yarn to make clothes for the family. Handloom weaving was then a thriving job for men in the country villages.

John Younger, Shoemaker, Autobiography, *1812.*

The Coming of the Factory

From 1750 the Cottage Industry could no longer make enough clothes for the increasing population. There was a need for cloth to be produced quickly and cheaply. Cotton cloth could now be made in large quantity by using spinning machines. But these machines were too big for farmers' cottages, and could only be put into factories. Before a cotton factory or mill could be built, several things had to be taken into account.

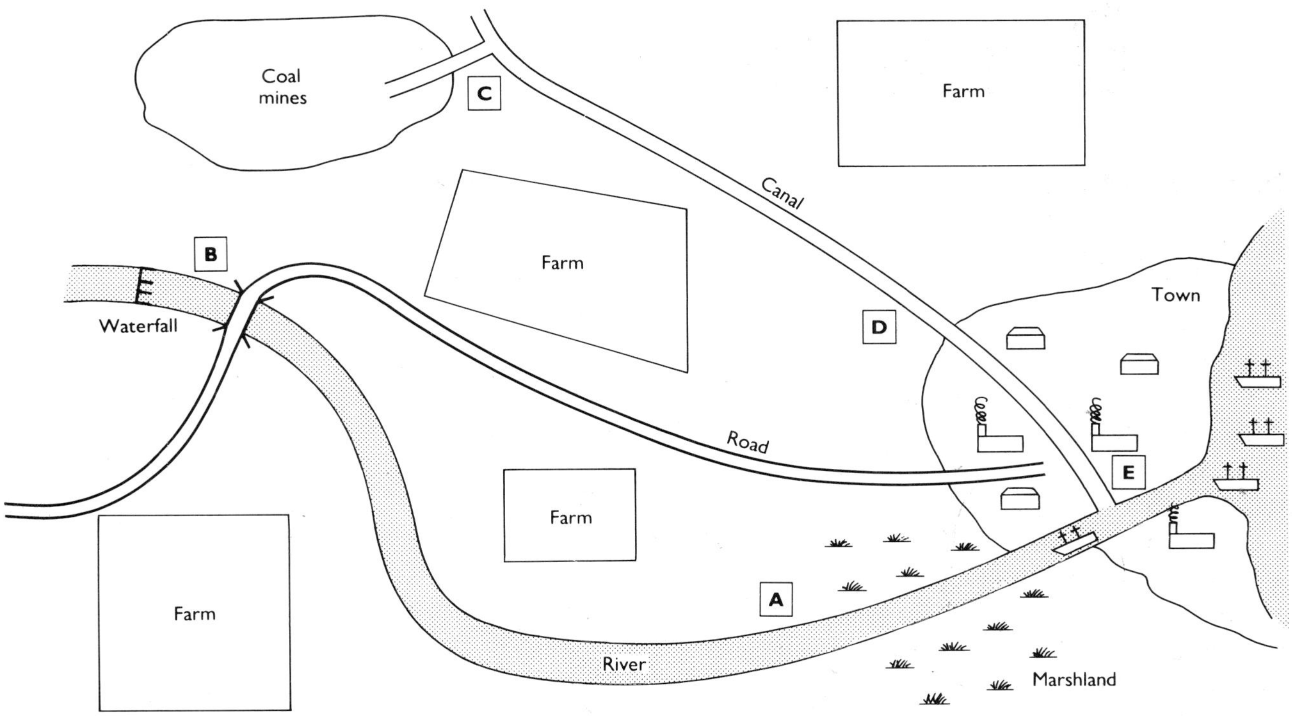

1. Town merchants or businessmen who would invest money to buy the spinning machines and build the factory.
2. Land to build the factory and houses for the workers.
3. Power for the machines. The first machines were driven by water power. The later steam driven machines also needed a lot of coal.
4. A good supply of workers nearby to operate the machines.
5. Good transport to take the raw cotton to the factory and the cloth away from the factory.

?

1 Describe in your own words how the Cottage Industry worked.
Pair work: In pairs, discuss and write down as many reasons as you can why the Cottage Industry was not very efficient.

2 Copy the diagram above into your workbooks.
Group work: You are hired as consultants by a group of businessmen to choose the best site for a cotton factory. There are five possible sites marked A,B,C,D,E. In your group you should discuss each site, and write the good and bad points of each. The group should give each site a mark out of 10. Then write a report back to the businessmen saying which site you have chosen and the reasons for your choice.

KING COTTON

The coming of the factory system brought about a rapid expansion of the cotton industry in Britain, especially in Lancashire and the West of Scotland. The Clyde valley was particularly suitable for the manufacture of cotton because:

- The climate was mild and damp enough to prevent the threads from snapping.
- There were plenty of rivers for water power.
- The West Coast location was very convenient for the direct import of raw cotton from America.
- Workers already skilled in the linen trade could readily be employed in the manufacture of cotton.
- Rich tobacco merchants were anxious to invest their wealth in cotton.

In Scotland the first cotton mill was opened in Penicuik in Midlothian in 1778, and it was followed by another in Rothesay a year later. However, the large-scale production of cotton thread using Arkwright's Water Frame was begun by David Dale at the village of New Lanark in 1786, and he later opened other mills at Blantyre in Lanarkshire, Catrine in Ayrshire and Spinningdale in Sutherland. In fact, the partnership of Dale and Arkwright at New Lanark was so successful that within 10 years of opening the mill employed over 1,300 people.

Other businessmen saw the potential of cotton manufacture, and other mills were built at Neilston (1780), Johnstone (1782), East Kilbride and Woodside in Glasgow (1783).

Many of these sites were ideal for the full-scale production of cotton, as in the case of Greenock.

C The advantages possessed and expected by this cotton company in setting up business at Greenock are, a cheap and constant supply of water at all seasons, the Glasgow market, the possibility of attending the Liverpool markets by a sail of sixteen or seventeen hours; to which may be added an abundant population for carrying on the work and an excellent port for importing cotton, or exporting cotton yarns to the continent of India.

New Statistical Account, the Parish of Greenock.

The need for plentiful supplies of water to power the massive spinning machines resulted in most of the early mills being located in rural areas, where cotton towns were created. From around the year 1800 steam power was to take over, and most of the mills could be concentrated in large towns.

D Anchor Mills at Paisley

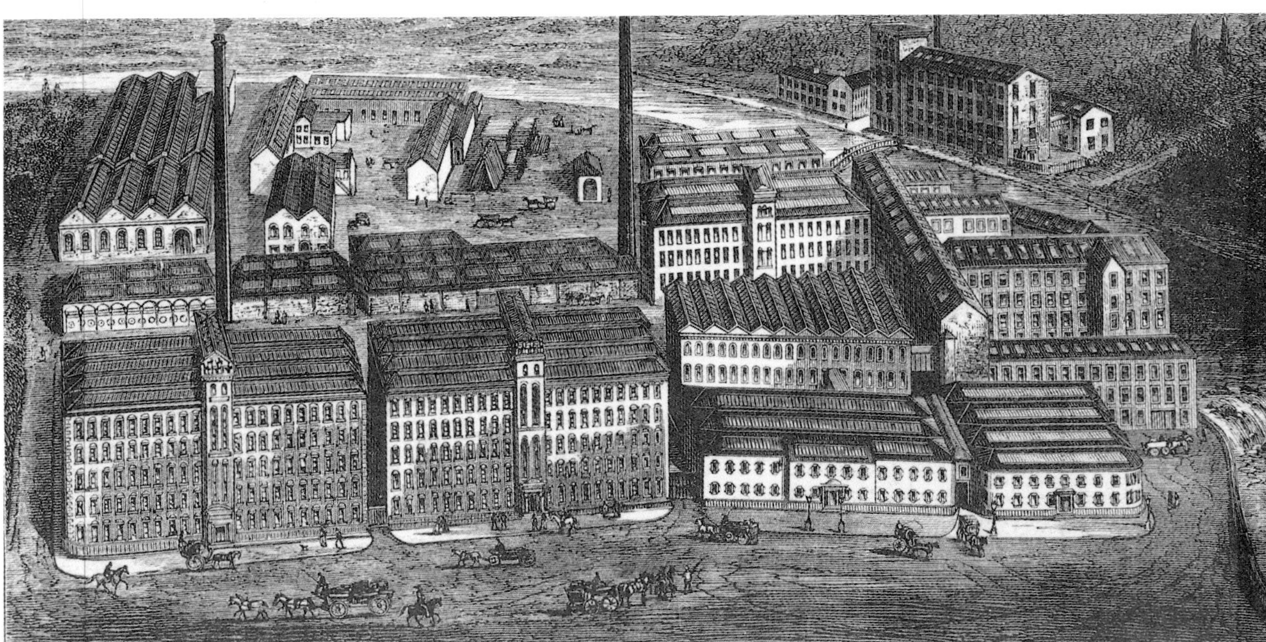

By 1800 cotton was undoubtedly the most flourishing industry in Scotland, and clearly deserved the title of 'King Cotton'. In 1812 there were 120 spinning mills in business, and by 1840 the number had risen to around 190. It is difficult to obtain precise statistics for the cotton industry, but it is estimated that the capital invested in cotton rose from £650,000 in 1790 to £4.5 million in 1840. Further, raw cotton imported into the Clyde rose from 137,160lb to 11,114,640lb between 1775 and 1812. The demand for cotton cloth came not only from Europe, America and the British Empire, but also from a growing home market, as cotton provided a cheap material for the growing population.

Case Study – Lochwinnoch

The Black Cart river became a very important factor in the economy of the area as cotton mills were built along its banks between Lochwinnoch and Linwood.

E 53 new houses have been built . . . and the population, the wealth and the industry of its inhabitants have been increased within a very short time . . . Its rapid increase has been principally occasioned by the building of two large cotton mills . . . The mill built by Messrs Johnstone and Company employs at present 240 people and when the machinery is completed will employ 600.

Old Statistical Account, the Parish of Lochwinnoch

Year	Population
1755	1530
1791	2613
1801	2955
1811	3514
1821	4130
1831	4515

It will be seen that the population has increased rapidly since 1791. The chief reason of which was the building of cotton mills about that time, and the stimulus which this gave to every other kind of business.

The young men and women employed in the cotton mills can afford to live and dress well. Those who endure the heat, fatigue and long confinement of the mills require a generous diet. They have generally butcher meat at dinner, and sometimes at breakfast.

The new mill was built by Messrs Fulton & Company in 1789. It stands on the banks of the Calder, by the waters of which it was wholly driven till a large addition was built to it in 1825, when a steam engine was constructed. The mill consists of five storeys and is lighted by 360 windows and 60 skylights. It consists of 25,224 spindles, which work 12,000lbs of cotton every fortnight.

It employs 345 workers who receive about £260 in wages in a fortnight. The persons employed in the cotton mills work 12 hours, five days in the week and nine hours on Saturday. They have one hour and forty minutes for both breakfast and dinner. The confinement and high temperature of the mills must enfeeble the body and ultimately tell upon the health of the workers.

New Statistical Account, the Parish of Lochwinnoch.

Although the coming of cotton mills brought many benefits to various communities, they also created many problems. Most mill buildings were unattractive. The mill at Johnstone was described as 'great gaunt buildings towering to many storeys of monotonous flats, their sides studded with regular rows of little windows'. The town of Johnstone had a total of 20 mills by 1838 which resulted in both the pollution of the rivers and the surrounding atmosphere.

Fire was a constant threat. In 1828 a fire broke out in the basement of Stewart's Mill in Johnstone, and with wooden stairs, wooden oil-saturated floors, and thousands of bails of cotton, it quickly spread to the other three floors. The workers on the top floor were trapped by the fire, and in all six people died and many others were seriously injured.

?

1. Promotional Booklet
   Make an attractive booklet designed to persuade businessmen to set up a cotton mill somewhere in Scotland.
2. Write a report giving the advantages and disadvantages of a cotton mill to a community like Lochwinnoch in the West of Scotland.

MORE AND MORE MACHINES

Around 1750 spinning was done by simple, hand-operated machines. They could produce only a single thread at a time (see page 28). But there was now a need to find a quicker method of spinning to produce more and more thread. It was soon discovered that a fast flow of water was strong enough to turn large water wheels, which in turn were able to drive all the machines in a factory.

F Water wheel – Cotton Mill at Cromford (Derbyshire)

This discovery meant that larger and more complex spinning machines could be developed.

Inventions

1765 – Hargreaves' Spinning Jenny
It could spin eight threads at once, but later models increased the number of threads to 120. The thread it produced was very fine and tended to snap easily.

G Spinning Jenny

1769 – Arkwright's Water Frame
This machine was much larger than the Jenny. It produced a much stronger thread. It could be driven only by water power and had to be placed in a factory.

1779 – Crompton's Mule
The Mule was able to produce a thread that was both soft and strong. By 1790 this machine could spin 300 threads at once.

From about 1790 steam-driven machines were introduced into the mills. A steam-driven Mule needed only one operator to control a total of 1,200 spindles at the same time. As a result, by around 1830 large numbers of skilled spinners were no longer needed.

Despite the invention of several spinning machines, until 1785 weaving was still done by hand. There was therefore plenty of work for the handloom weavers. In 1785 Cartwright invented

H Crompton's Mule

a weaving machine called the Power Loom. There were problems at first with this machine, and it was not until around 1820 that the power loom was used in large numbers.

The number of power looms in use in Britain

1820 =	14,000
1833 =	100,000
1850 =	250,000

The result was a great increase in the production of cotton cloth after 1820, although many handloom weavers lost their jobs.

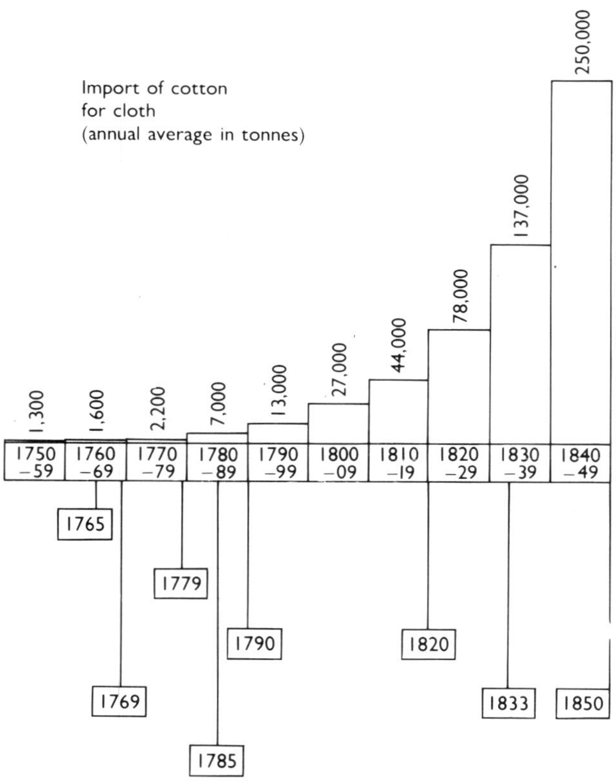

?

1 Copy the outline of the bar graph showing the amount of imported cotton which was made into cotton cloth in Britain. Colour in the bars of your graph in red.
Now make up a time line using the eight dates at the bottom of the graph. Next to each date write a sentence explaining the importance of that date.

2 Group Work
Discuss and write down the main reasons for the success of the cotton industry in Scotland between 1750 and 1850. Also the group should note down any examples of how people might have been badly affected by the development of cotton. Then write a short speech under the title of King Cotton.

THE RISE AND FALL OF THE WEAVERS

Towards the end of the eighteenth century, the rapidly increasing numbers of powerful spinning machines in the cotton mills were producing large quantities of thread ready to be woven into cloth. At this time the process of weaving could only be done effectively by hand by individual weavers in their own cottages. Although the numbers of handloom weavers increased considerably at this time – in 1790 it was estimated that there were 45,000 weavers in Scotland and this number rose to around 84,000 by 1840 – there was still too much demand for their work. As a result, the weavers could demand high wages for their work. At a time when a good average weekly wage was around 10 shillings (50p) for six days work, the weavers were able to make from 30s to 40s (£1.50 to £2) for a four-day week. It was for this reason that the handloom weavers were known as the 'Aristocrats of Labour'. The lifestyle of the weavers was the envy of all other workers.

1 The Weaver's House, Kilbarchan

J Four days did the weaver work, for them four days was a week . . . and such a week to a skilled workman brought forty shillings. Sunday, Monday and Tuesday were of course days of celebration. Fine linen frills came out from under the wrists of his fine blue, gilt buttoned coat. He dusted his head with white flour on Sunday, smirked, and wore a cane. Walked in clean slippers on Monday. Tuesday heard him talk war bravado . . . and get drunk. Weaving commenced gradually on Wednesday.

William Thom, Rhymes and Recollections of a Handloom Weaver

However, the days of propsperity for the handloom weaver were coming to an end. In 1787 a clergyman called Edmund Cartwright invented a power loom which could weave the cotton thread into cloth much faster and at half the cost of a man on the handloom. Although the power loom was first used in Scotland as early as 1793, there were initial technical difficulties with Cartwright's loom and it took some time before it was adopted in the industry. In 1807 James Findlay and Company introduced an improved power loom into their factory in Catrine, but it was not until the 1830s that power looms, now driven by steam in place of the earlier water power, were installed in most cotton factories.

The number of power looms in use in Scotland

1820 =	2,000
1830 =	10,000
1853 =	19,000
1845 =	23,000

The power loom brought distress to the handloom weaver, but his disappearance was both slow and painful. There was now not sufficient work for the weaver, and although some were able to produce fine work for which the power loom was unsuitable, the number of weavers fell from 84,000 in 1840 to only 25,000 by 1850. The high wages were no longer available and the average weekly income fell from around £2 to about 10 shillings (50p) at the most. Many weavers had to content themselves with wages as low as 4s to 8s (20p to 40p). More and more weavers were reduced to living in appalling poverty as some of the poorest members of the communities of Glasgow, Renfrewshire and Ayrshire.

K The Power Loom, 1834

L A very great number of the weavers are unable to provide for themselves and their families enough food for the plainest and cheapest kind; they are clothed in rags, they have scarcely anything like furniture in their houses, their beds and bedding are of the most wretched description, many of them sleep upon straw; notwithstanding their want, they have full employment, but their labour is exececessive, not infrequently 16 hours a day.

Report of Hand-loom Weavers Committee (1835), Parliamentary Papers.

But the distress of the handloom weaver was caused by factors other than the power loom. In the first half of the ninteenth century there was an influx of workers from Ireland and the Highlands into the weaving trade. Many of these new weavers were content to accept lower wages and poorer conditions than those who had been used to a better life.

M The Irish weavers are the main cause of pulling the Scotch down after them. Of course they are in a slightly better condition than in their own country, which is precisely the reason why they take the lead in the career downhill, having less natural opposition to poverty which they have been in some measure previously used to. When a Master desires to lower his wages it is likely that the Irish were first to accept his terms.

Report on Handloom Weavers, 1840

Like the Luddites in England, in 1812 weavers in Scotland tried to protect their livelihood by smashing power looms in the mills at Catrine and Deanston. Also that year, weavers in the Calton district of Glasgow went on strike when their employers tried to reduce their wages. The weavers continued to cause trouble in the 1820s and 1830s, hoping to restrict the number of people coming into the weaving trade and attempting to keep up the price of woven cloth, but by the depression years of 1841-3 and 1848 the golden years of the handloom weaver had gone forever.

?

1. Evaluation
   What evidence is contained in source J to support the view that the handloom weaver lived a comfortable life in the late-eighteenth century? Similarly, what evidence does source L contain to show distress by 1835?
2. James Smith worked as a handloom weaver in Paisley from 1806 to 1838. His rise and fall can be seen through his wages; he earned £54.30p in 1811 and only £33.31p in 1838. You have been asked to write his biography, making use of sources I–M. You should divide your life story of James Smith into three parts: The Years of Prosperity – The Reasons for Decline – The Years of Distress.
3. According to source M, why did the arrival of the Irish adversely affect the position of the handloom weavers in Scotland?

THE FACTORY CHILDREN

N Cotton Mill Children

By 1830 large numbers of children were employed in the cotton mills. Many families were so poor that even very young children were sent out to work. They were often taken on as scavengers, crawling underneath the machines, cleaning and oiling them as they went. Older children worked as piecers, watching the hundreds of threads and joining together those that broke. Young men became spinners, operating the large machines.

The working conditions in most factories were dreadful. By the early 1830s the Government sent out inspectors to find out how bad it really was. These inspectors talked to both young and adult workers, as well as the factory owners.

O Elizabeth Bentley (23, Leeds) began work at the age of six in Mr Busk's mill . . . Hours 5 am till 9 pm when they were busy, otherwise 6 am till 9 pm, with 40 minutes for meal at noon.

Anne Campbell (16, Dundee) earns 4/6 (22p) a week . . . is too tired to go to school of an evening.

John Gibb (11, Glasgow) says the spinners often hit him with a strap of leather.

James Brownlie – Mill Manager (Glasgow) No beating of a boy or girl is allowed in this factory.

Peter Buchanan (19, Paisley) There is a great deal of dust at the work he is at, that makes him very hoarse, and often to cough, and he is sometimes very short of breath . . . the long standing gives him pains at night in the ankles.

Isabella Simson (13, Kirkcaldy) I stand in the wet and my feet are so swelled and red, my hands are all cut with the warm water.

Boy from Bradford (16) We always have to bend our bodies and legs. Within a year, my legs became crooked. I have to stand with crutches, or a stick, or lean against something.

I once saw a boy get his arm entangled in a machine. Both his feet were knocked off, his arm was broken in three places; he lived for 24 hours after the accident, and then died.

Peter Pollock – Mill Manager in Paisley Workers have never worked longer than thirteen hours . . . he divides the meal hours, at the request of the workers themselves, into three quarters of an hour each for breakfast and dinner. Only remembers two accidents in twenty years. Never had a single complaint during the twenty years by any child or parent.

Report on Employment of Children in Factories, 1833

P Inspectors at work

?

1. Five people in source N are given a number. Against each number in your workbooks, put in which you think is the mill owner: scavenger: piecer: spinner: overseer (foreman).
2. What evidence is there in source N of poverty among the children in the mill?
3. Write down what the workers had to say in source O about life in the mills under the following headings: age starting work : hours of work : discipline : health : accidents : wages.
4. There are also two reports on what the mill owners thought about life in the mill. Write down three ways in which they did not agree with what the workers said.

GOOD AND BAD FACTORIES

At the beginning of the nineteenth century, people were becoming more and more aware of the appalling conditions in many textile factories in Britain. Although it was felt that adult workers had the choice whether to endure factory life or not, there was growing concern about the effect on the health and welfare of children. Many people in fact saw nothing wrong in children working a twelve-hour day; in one factory it was noted that young children were 'as healthy stout people as any in the country'. However, the alternative view was that most children were forced to work in the mills, either by their parents or orphanages, and that both the bad conditions and cruel treatment undoubtedly injured their health.

Conditions became so bad in many textile factories that Parliament was persuaded to set up a Royal Commission in 1832. The result was to send Commissioners all over Britain to ask both workers and owners about the working conditions for children. Controversy resulted as some Commissioners found evidence in favour of the employers while others supported the workers.

Here are the actual reports of some of these Government Commissioners.

Q Gilchrist's Mill at Inverbervie
It is dirty, low roofed, ill ventilated, ill drained; no conveniences for carrying off dust; machinery not boxed in, passages so narrow that they could hardly be defined; some of the flats so low that it is scarcely possible to stand upright in the centre of the rooms. The house of Gilchrist the mill owner, presented a picture of filth and want of comfort of every kind, such as I have rarely seen elsewhere.

Parliamentary Papers, 1833

S In Archibald Buchanan's Mill at Catrine I had great pleasure in walking through the eighteen apartments of the spinning mill and witnessing the admirable order of the works, and the apparent happiness of the people employed. The windows open from the top; the rooms are thoroughly ventilated; there is a clock and thermometer in every room; no unpleasant smell in any part of the work, and the utmost cleanness and neatness prevailing throughout. The works are well provided with fans, and the inconveniences from dust has been thoroughly removed.

Parliamentary Papers, 1833

T Margaret Wilson (20) – worker at a mill in Perthshire
She has been in the mill ever since she can recollect anything . . . she now makes 6s (30p) a week; that since she went to the mill she has always been hoarse and had pains in her chest, and her feet and ankles swell very much with standing so long; that she has had no time to go to school here, that her father taught her to read some, but she can't write.

Parliamentary Papers, 1833

R Factory slaves – a contemporary cartoon

U Alexander Dean – worker from Dundee
Were the children kept to their work by punishment?
Yes.
What were they beaten with generally?
Sometimes the master's son would take a strap, or if the master himself was about the work, and saw a small fault, he struck them both with his hands and feet.
Does loss of life and limb occur due to the excessive labour which those children are forced to undergo?
I had one girl under my charge: she could not see very well, and towards evening . . . she was drowsy and sleepy and her thumb came into contact with the machinery. I heard the snap, and by the time I came to her, her thumb was away from her hand, and so she held out her hand to me with the thumb missing.

Parliamentary Papers, 1833

V Medical Report on J & J Clark Cotton Mill in Paisley
The number of workers in this mill is 107. There is only one girl so young as thirteen; there is one boy of nine, and one of eleven years of age; no other male under fourteen. All the workers appear to be in health, and look fresh in colour. James Balderstone, overseer for sixteen years, declares that he never knew any worker become deformed at this mill. There have been no accidents from the machinery in the last twelve months. Only four workers have died in the last sixteen years.

Factories Commission, 1833

The reports of the various Commissioners convinced most MPs that something had to be done to control the employment of children in the factories. On 29 August 1833 the Factory Reform Act introduced by Lord Althorpe passed through Parliament and became law.

Terms of the Factory Act

- The employment of children under 9 years of age banned.
- Children between 9 and 13 to work only 8 hours a day, with an additional 2 hours schooling.
- Children between 13 and 16 to work only 69 hours a week.
- Night work banned for those under 18.
- Children not to clean machinery while it was in motion.
- Minimum meal breaks of 1½ hours a day for all children.
- Four factory inspectors appointed to enforce the Act.
- Factory owners to keep a register of all children.

Later Factory Acts improved conditions even further. In 1844 Graham's Factory Act reduced the minimum age to eight, but at the same time set a maximum 6½-hour day for those children under 13 and 12 hours a day for boys and girls under 18. In 1847 Fielden's Act finally reduced the working day to 10 hours for all women and children under 18 years.

?

1. Evaluation
How effective and reliable are sources Q to V in giving us a clear idea about what life in the textile factories was really like?
2. Group taped interview
Each group of three pupils should decide who is to adopt the role of the interviewer, a Commissioner who visited a well-run factory, and a Commissioner who visited a dreadful factory. The interviewer should ask both Commissioners the same six questions, and all questions and answers should be recorded on tape.
3. Write a short report on how effective you think the 1833 Reform Act was in improving the conditions in the cotton mills.

A MODEL FACTORY – New Lanark

In 1783 David Dale, a wealthy Glasgow banker, and Richard Arkwright, an English inventor, decided to build a cotton mill at the Falls of Clyde near Lanark. It was an ideal site, as the fast flowing waters of the Clyde would provide the power to drive Arkwright's new spinning machines. The first mill building was finished by April 1785. But the river was very twisty at New Lanark, and Dale was forced to build a 300-yard tunnel or lade to lead the water from the Clyde to the water wheels of the mill.

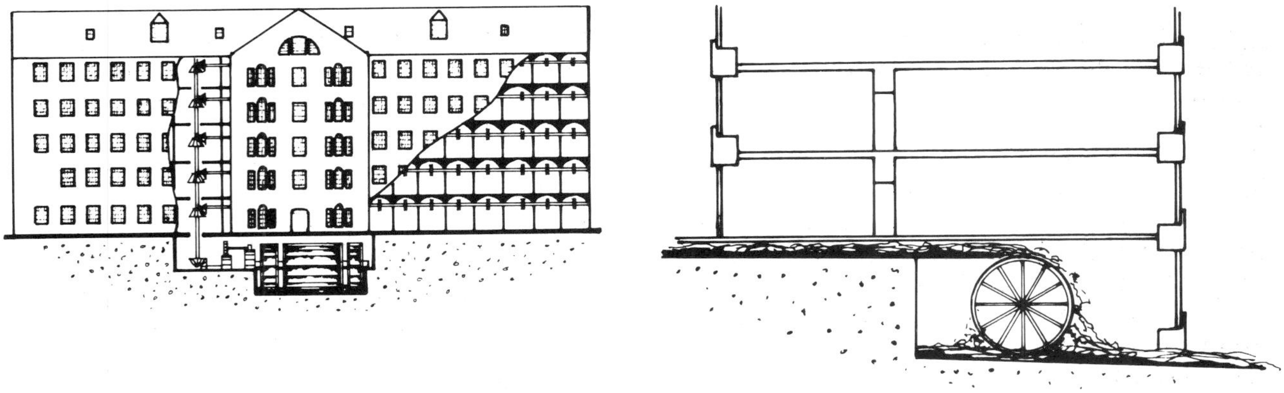

W The Mill Lade

Spinning began at New Lanark in March 1786, but there were not enough adult workers in the local area. Dale was forced to take on large numbers of children from orphanages in Glasgow and Edinburgh. However, in the early 1790s he was able to persuade several Highland families to settle and work in New Lanark rather than emigrate to America. By 1793 there were 1,187 people at New Lanark, of which around 800 were young boys or girls, and by 1799 the total number had risen to 2,500.

In 1799 David Dale's daughter Caroline married a Welshman called Robert Owen, who immediately took over the running of the mill. During the next 25 years, Owen was able to make large profits from the New Lanark mills, but at the same time he gained a reputation for caring for the workers.

X New Lanark 1818

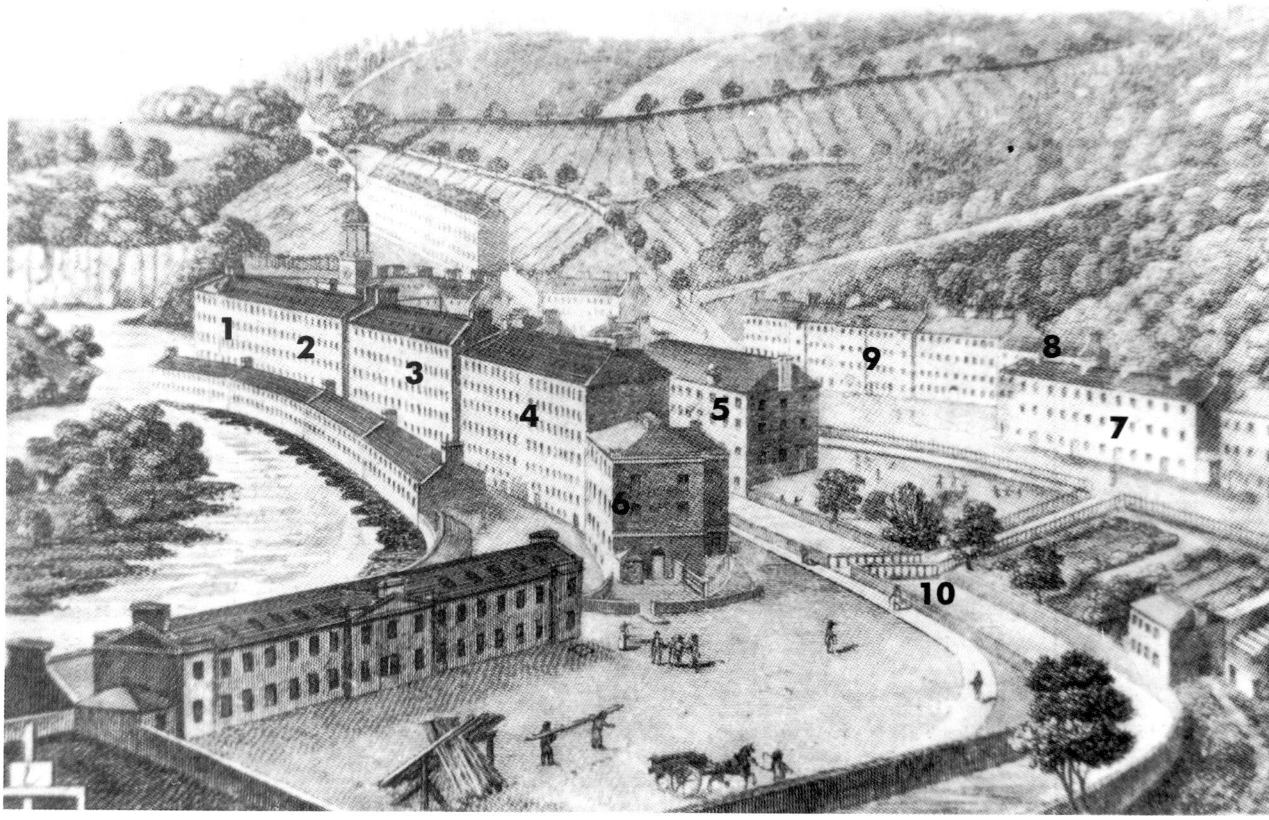

Y New Lanark 1820

This is what the New Lanark community looked like by about 1820.

Key to the picture

1. Mill
2.
3.
4.

No children under 10 were allowed to work in the mills. There was no beating of the workers allowed. Most workers worked 12 hours a day, with with 1 hour 15 minutes for meals.

5. The Institute for the Formation of Character – It was built in 1816 at a cost of £3,000 and was the social centre of the village. It contained rooms for books and games, and was later used as a dance and music hall.
6. School — It was finished in 1817 for all the children of the village from five to ten years of age. They were taught to read and write, but also to sing and dance.
7. Housing — Rows of well built tenement houses for all the workers of the mill. Each house was made up of a single room for an entire family, but they were inspected to see if they were kept clean.
8. Store — It was started in 1813 and goods were sold to the workers almost at cost price.
9. Nursery — Built in 1809 to house the small orphan children.
10. Lade

?

1 David Dale had two main problems when he started the mill at New Lanark.
1) How to get the water from the Clyde to the mills.
2) How to get enough workers for the mills.
Explain how he solved both these problems.

2 Speech
Write a short speech for the rest of the class on the topic: "Why you would prefer to work at New Lanark than in any other mill in Scotland".

THE GREAT EXPERIMENT

On 1 January 1800 Robert Owen took over the management of the New Lanark mills. At first, the workers did not welcome the arrival of Owen; the hours of work were soon increased from 12 to 14 hours a day, and each person's work was to be supervised constantly. It was clear that Owen was determined to make the New Lanark mills run at a profit. However, in 1806 the workers were to see Owen's generosity as he continued to pay them full wages for several months when the mills were forced to close following a sharp rise in the price of raw cotton from America.

Robert Owen now decided to introduce many of his reforming ideas to bring about a more benevolent system of management in New Lanark. He believed that the welfare of the workers was very important, and that good education and good housing, as well as good discipline, would result in a contented and efficient workforce. He hated the exploitation of child workers and the squalid working conditions that existed in most cotton factories in Britain. Owen was able to prove that looking after the welfare of his workers could go hand in hand with financial success.

By the early years of the nineteenth century, New Lanark was one of the largest and most profitable mills in Britain. Owen kept a close record of productivity, and he also introduced a Silent Monitor system in which a four-sided piece of wood was placed next to each worker to indicate his performance according to the following code: Black for Bad, Blue for Indifferent, Yellow for Good and White for Excellent.

Robert Owen was concerned about the welfare of all his workers and their families, and in 1831 he described the conditions he had established at New Lanark in this way.

Z The practice of employing children in the mills, of six, seven and eight years of age, was discontinued, and their parents advised to allow them to acquire health and education until they were ten years old . . . The children were taught reading, writing and arithmetic from five to ten in the village school, without expense to their parents. Their houses were rendered more comfortable, their streets were improved, the best food was purchased, and sold to them at low rates . . . fuel and clothes were obtained for them in the same manner . . . Those employed became industrious, temperate, healthy, faithful to their employers, and kind to each other.

Robert Owen, A New View of Society, *1831*

Owen also set up a Sick Fund into which each worker contributed one-sixtieth of their wages. But, Robert Owen's greatest legacy was in the field of education. Owen believed that people were not born either good or bad, but that their character was formed in their youth by their

AA School at New Lanark

environment. As soon as they could walk, the children were taken into the nursery, which allowed their mothers to work in the mill. Children up to the age of ten went to the day school from 7.30 am to 5 pm (10 am to 2 pm in the winter) where 14 teachers taught about 270 pupils the basics of reading, writing and arithmetic and also singing, dancing, sewing, nature study, drawing, history, geography and science. Older children were brought in to take evening classes between 7 pm to 9 pm.

Robert Owen encouraged dancing and singing which attracted several visitors to his school.

BB These children, standing up 70 couples at a time in the dancing room and often surrounded with many visitors would, with the utmost elegance and natural grace, go through all the dances of Europe . . . In their singing lessons 150 would sing at the same time, their voices trained to harmonise, and it was delightful to hear them singing the old popular Scotch songs.

Robert Owen, A New View of Society, *1831*

The school also looked after the health of the children by running out-of-doors lessons in the summer, either in the large school playground or walks around the village. Children were encouraged to bring objects like flowers, stones and even animals for study in the class-rooms. Neither physical punishment nor even harsh words had any place in Owen's ideal world at New Lanark.

In addition, Owen made sure that all children had sufficient food and clothing. Pauper children were provided with cotton suits in the summer and woollen ones in the winter months, as well as a dress-suit for Sundays. These clothes were washed regularly. Special tunics were given to the children for school. Their diet consisted of beef or cheese with barley broth, potatoes, barley bread, oatmeal porridge with milk, and occasionally fresh herrings were served as a change. Although the food was fairly substantial it was both plain and monotonous.

Robert Owen's model factory and village at New Lanark gained international praise, but his experiment came to an end when Owen and his son left for America in 1824. A year later Owen broke his link with New Lanark altogether.

?

1. Imagine that you are Robert Owen, how would you answer the following questions in a radio interview?
   How did you manage to obtain the loyalty and happiness of your workers?
   How did you succeed in making the factory a financial success?
   Why do you think education is so important?
   How did you make the village school so attractive?
   Why do you think so many visitors wanted to come and see New Lanark?
   How did you look after the pauper children?
2. How effectively do sources Z, AA and BB reflect Robert Owen's ideas on education?

5 THE GROWTH OF TOWNS

Larger towns

In 1750 most of the Clyde Valley was farmland. There were a few towns and villages. The only large town was Glasgow, which had grown in size due to wealth from the tobacco trade with America.

By 1850 the Clyde Valley had changed completely. Much of the farmland disappeared as thousands of people came into the Valley to work in the new factories. Towns like Paisley grew in size and population.

Population of the Counties of Lanark and Renfrew

	1755	1801	1821
Lanark	81,726	147,692	244,387
Renfrew	26,645	78,501	112,175

?

1 Make a list of ways the Clyde Valley changed between 1750 and 1850 under the following headings:
Population: Industry: Towns.

2 Make a bar graph showing the growth of the population in Lanarkshire and Renfrewshire.

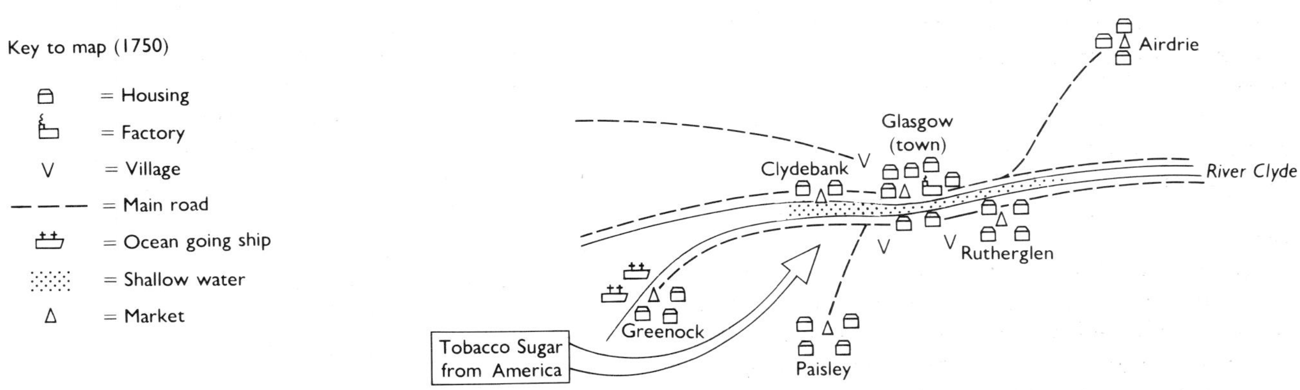

Clyde Valley, 1750

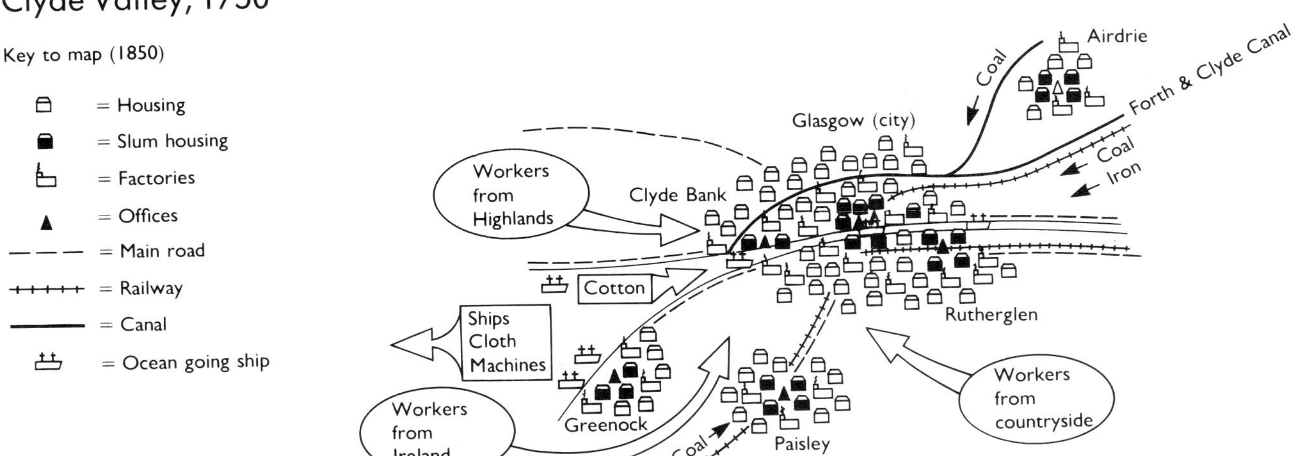

Clyde Valley, 1850

CASE STUDY – Glasgow

The growth of Glasgow was the most spectacular of all the Clyde Valley towns. After the Treaty of Union (1707) Glasgow merchants had access to the tobacco trade with English colonies in America. This brought tremendous wealth to the city and its merchant class. When the tobacco trade collapsed in 1775, these merchants were easily able to transfer their capital into other industrial ventures.

In the years between 1775 and 1850 Glasgow developed as a centre for cotton manufacture as well as the heavy industries of coal, iron, engineering and shipbuilding. Glasgow's skyline was littered with the chimneys of hundreds of factories.

To allow ocean-going ships direct access to Glasgow's industrial centre in 1773 John Golborne succeeded in deepening the River Clyde to a depth of 7 feet at low tide, and to 14 feet by 1781.

Different features of the expansion of the city of Glasgow in the century after 1750 are shown in the sources below.

A Glasgow c1760 – A provincial town

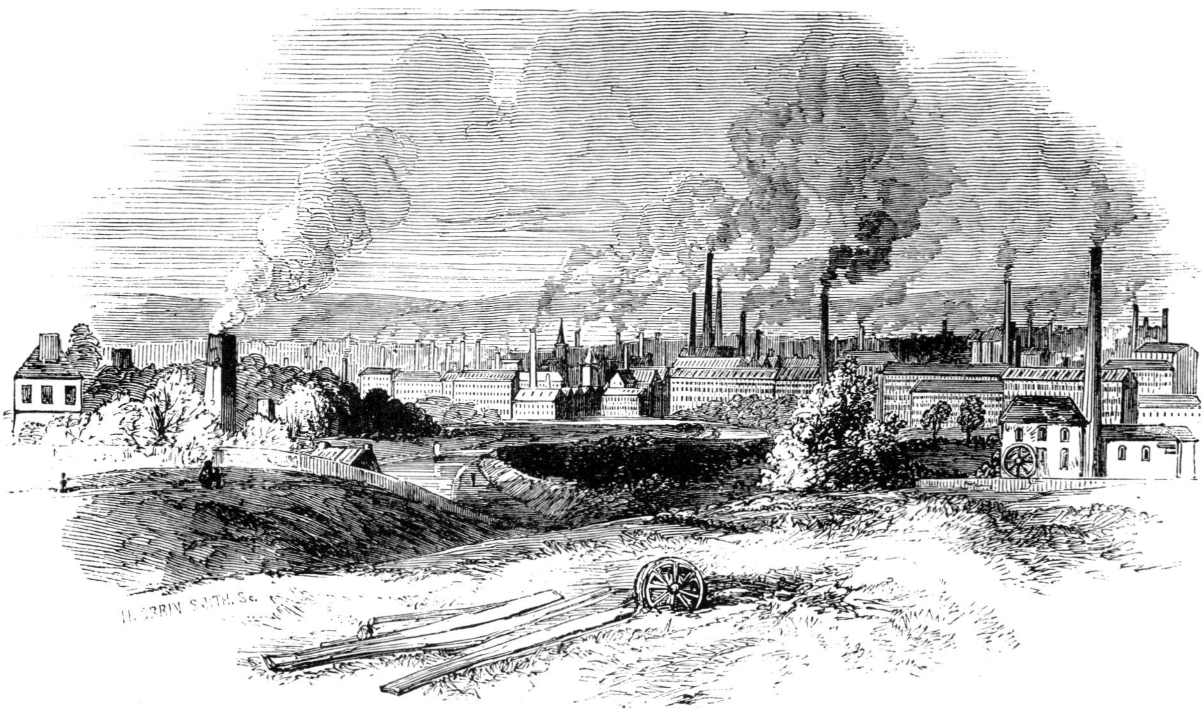

B Glasgow c1835 – An industrial city

C The old town lay chiefly beneath the cathedral. The new town gradually descended from the old one to the river, the source of its commerce and its prosperity. Having at length reached the Clyde, it continued spreading eastwards along its banks, and now taking in the village of Anderston, it extends over two miles in length. Every part of this large space is not equally covered with houses at present; but probably will in a few years. The rate of building perhaps out-runs the increase of inhabitants, now computed at sixty thousand.

I Lettice, Tour, Scots Magazine, *1794*

D During the past few years green paths where cattle grazed and greens where housewives bleached their clothes have been almost covered with houses, there has been much building of late of tenements for workmen's houses. During the past season in the north west districts there have been erected 1,069 separate dwelling houses, about 800 of which are suitable for working men. In the east of the city whole streets of dwelling houses have been erected within the past few years. Still the supply is insufficient to meet the requirements of the increasing population.

Glasgow Herald, 1870

E

Birthplace of residents of Glasgow, 1851

Highlands	North East	Lowlands	Borders
5.2%	0.8%	26.6%	1.8%

Ireland	Rest of UK	Glasgow
8.2%	3.1%	44.1%

1851 Census, Parliamentary Papers

F

Occupations of people in Glasgow

Engineering	=	7%
Building Trade	=	6%
Textiles	=	38%
General Labouring	=	8%
Food and drink	=	5%

1841 Census, Parliamentary Papers

?

1. Using sources A to F, present a report stating how Glasgow expanded in the 100 years from 1750 to 1850. You can develop your report into an investigation on the expansion of Glasgow, or do a similar investigation on your own town, by using other sources or books.
2. Compare the evidence about the growth of Glasgow in sources C and D.

*T*HE GROWTH OF SLUMS

As thousands of poor families flooded into the towns and cities of Britain in search of work, the main problem was to find homes for these people close to their place of work. In most industrial towns the solution was to construct tenement style buildings. But, as most of these workers were unskilled and poor, they were probably able to afford little more than a single-room flat. Therefore, as the population of these towns rapidly increased, overcrowding became a major problem.

Most of the tenements were owned by private landlords who were happy to cram as many families as possible into their homes. Many such dwellings were built around 1800, and by 1850 they had fallen into bad repair. Most landlords did little to improve their property, and consequently the urban workers were forced to live in shocking conditions. These areas were given the appropriate name of slums.
Some of the worst slums in Britain were to be found in the centre of Glasgow.

G 65 High Street, Glasgow

Although the photograph above was taken in 1868, it shows clearly the housing conditions during the first half of the nineteenth century. In 1849 Dr Sutherland described these terrible conditions during his visits to the houses along the High Street.

H They are made up of rows of narrow closes, only some four or five feet wide but very long. The houses are so high that the direct light of the sun never reaches most of the dwellings. Ordinary ventilation is impossible. There are large midden boxes, some of them actually under the houses, and all of them close to the windows and doors of the houses. These boxes hold the entire filth of large numbers of people, until farmers can be persuaded to remove the rubbish. There is no drainage in these areas, and because there is no means of flushing, the sewers, where they do exist, are large cesspools (pools of filthy water) polluting the air. On one occasion I saw the entire surface of a backyard covered for several inches with green stinking water. The common stairs and passages of the houses are often the site of the most disgusting filth. The houses themselves are dark, and without any ventilation. The walls are falling down and filthy. There are no toilets even in the highest tenements. There is a kind of wooden sink placed outside some stair windows, and it is connected by a square wooden pipe with the surface of the close or court below. Down this pipe is poured the entire filth of the household to which it belongs, and solid rubbish frequently goes the same way until the pipe becomes blocked.

Dr Sutherland, Report on the Measures Adopted for the Relief of Cholera in Glasgow during the Epidemic of 1848-9, *1849*

Such slum conditions were not only in Glasgow. Most towns in Scotland had their slum areas. These houses in the Grassmarket in Edinburgh were already old by 1850.

I Grassmarket in Edinburgh

?

1. Group Work
   A group should have four pupils. Decide who will take the role of the interviewer, Dr Sutherland, a factory worker, and his wife. Then write a script for a series of interview questions to both Dr Sutherland and the slum family. The interview should be recorded on tape, and played to the whole class.
2. Assess how reliable sources G, H, and I are for historians trying to find out what slum life was really like around 1850.

LIVING AND DYING

In 1839 the Government set up an investigation to find out what life was really like in the slums in British towns and cities. Thousands of people had died from different types of killer diseases and nobody knew what caused them.

Edwin Chadwick was put in charge of this investigation, and he asked the doctors who worked in the slums to send him reports about the living conditions. Here are some of these reports.

J *London*
People got their water from a well in the courts. The people have only a small supply of water in their tubs.
Liverpool
I found the whole court knee-deep in fluid filth which oozed through the walls from two cesspools (a pit dug below the toilet).
Glasgow
There are no privies or drains, and the dunghills received all the filth which the wretched inhabitants could give; and we learnt that much of of the rent of the houses was paid by the produce of dunghills.
Greenock
In the summer each house swarms with flies. Food and drink left uncovered is made unfit for eating by the strong taste of the dunghill left by the flies.

Behind my room there is a large dunghill with a toilet attached; to my knowledge the dunghill has not been emptied for six months.
Edinburgh
The dwellings of the poor are normally very filthy . . . often of only one small apartment, always badly ventilated . . . many of them damp. Many of the poorest make up a kind of bed on the floor with straw, on which the whole family huddle together, some naked and others in the same clothes they have worn during the day.
Aberdeen
I have seen seven or eight sleeping in one tiny room, and I have more than once been nearly suffocated on entering.

Parliamentary Papers, 1842

In these conditions it is hardly surprising that death was everywhere in the slums. Chadwick himself said from his various reports that 'death from fever is greater in Glasgow, Edinburgh and Dundee than in the most crowded towns of England.' But what were the fevers that killed so many?

K Slum Life

Disease	Cause
Typhus	Virus carried from person to person by lice or fleas in poor, overcrowded conditions.
Cholera	Sewage seeping into the water supply, and people then drinking the infected water from wells.
T.B.	Germs coughed or sneezed into the air were breathed in by another person in a crowded room.
Typhoid	Eating infected food.

There were frequent outbreaks of these diseases after 1800. The result was a steady rise in the death rate. In Glasgow, for instance, 25 people in every 1,000 died in the 1820s, but between 1845 and 1849 40 people in every 1,000 were dying of these diseases.

But were children more likely to die in the slums than adults? Look at the tables of figures below to find out.

L

Deaths in Glasgow	Age
1026	Under 1
747	1 to 4
435	5 to 19
476	20 to 39
426	40 to 59
580	Over 60

Register of Burials of the City of Glasgow, 1822

M

Diseases of children under 10 who died in Glasgow (1791 and 1812)

	smallpox	measles	whooping cough	scarlet fever	bowel disease
1791	607	4	117	132	129

1796 Edward Jenner discovered vaccination to stop the spread of Smallpox.
1801 Doctors in Glasgow started vaccinating the poor children free of charge.

	smallpox	measles	whooping cough	scarlet fever	bowel disease
1812	78	304	103	105	279

James Cleland, Statistical and Population Tables relative to the City of Glasgow, *1828*

People were shocked by the findings in Chadwick's Report, and in 1848 the Government set up Boards of Health in England to force Town Councils to install proper drains, toilets and water supplies. But Health Boards already existed in many Scottish towns. Greenock had supplies of fresh water pumped through the town and Glasgow began removing the dunghills and old tenements in 1843.

?

1. Using sources J and K, make a list of the reasons why disease spread so easily in the slums.
2. Use evidence from source J to show why slums were ideal for the spread of each of these diseases: Typhus: Cholera: Typhoid: TB (Tuberculosis).
3. How difficult was it to survive as a young child in Glasgow in the early nineteenth century? Use the evidence in sources L and M to help you.

KING CHOLERA

The most feared of all the early nineteenth century slum diseases was undoubtedly cholera; a disease from Asia which made its British appearance in Sunderland in October 1831. From there it spread rapidly throughout the country. This first epidemic of 1831-2 claimed an estimated total of 10,000 lives in both large cities and small towns in Scotland.

The Sunderland Board of Health issued an official description of the disease.

N The early symptoms of the disease are giddiness, sick stomach, slow or small pulse, cramp at the top of fingers and toes.

Vomiting and purging (diarrhoea) of a liquid like rice water . . . the face becomes shrunken, the eyes sink and look wild, the whole body appears leaden, blue, purple, black . . .

The skin is deadly cold and often damp, the tongue always moist . . . breathing is often quick but irregular.

Sunderland Herald, 1831

Death would normally follow fairly quickly after the onset of these symptoms.

O A Sunderland girl dies of Cholera

The impact of cholera was frequently devastating; in 1832 it lasted in Glasgow from February to November.

P During that period there were 6,208 cases and 3,005 deaths. In the first outbreak, poorly fed persons who were dwelling in the crowded, ill-aired parts of the city, were chiefly affected.

The second outbreak was more severe, the attacks scattered over the town. Many healthy persons, in comfortable circumstances, fell victims to the disease.

New Statistical Account, Glasgow, 1835

The disease also struck other urban slums, as in Paisley where in 49 days there were 413 recorded cases of cholera, of whom 228 died. Yet, it was not just the horrible symptoms and numbers of dead that worried people and authorities, but the fact that the cause of the disease was unknown. Various doctors put forward different theories about how cholera spread.

- contact with the body or clothes of an infected person.
- breathing in the bad air from the filthy streets.
- spread by the smells coming from the body of an infected person.
- drunkenness could lead to an attack of cholera.

It was very difficult for doctors of the day to obtain evidence to support their own theory. For instance, it was noticed that the first death from cholera in Pollokshaws in 1848 was from the same bed in which it broke out in 1832, yet when some patients had to share a bed with cholera victims in Glasgow Town Hospital they did not seem to catch the disease.

Prevention

Various desperate measures were taken in towns and cities in Britain to try and halt the progress of cholera.

The Paisley Board of Health tried to get rid of the sources of cholera in the following ways:

- more scavengers to get rid of the piles of rubbish.
- slime covered ponds were pumped out.
- the poor given free soap.
- free lime to wash the walls of houses.
- ditches and burns cleaned out.
- foul smelling parts of the town fumigated.

Q

NOTICE

"That all Persons dying of Cholera, be buried within Twelve Hours after their decease, at latest; and that their Graves be dug not less than of the depth of Six Feet, if possible, and in Ground to be set apart for that purpose only."

Public Notice for Burial Regulations, Sunderland, 1831

The Edinburgh Health Board made the following suggestions:

R The Board would advise all persons to go out as little as possible at night during the epidemic . . . to clothe themselves more warmly than usual . . . to take care to keep their feet always warm and dry.

Edinburgh Board of Health, 1832

Most doctors still advised the traditional cure of bloodletting, but to no effect. In Paisley recorded cases of cholera were forced into hospital, and there the victims were treated with opium and hot mustard patches on the body, but the doctors also gave the victims regular, small amounts of salt and water. This treatment lessened the effect of dehydration (loss of body fluid), and as a result there was a better chance of recovery.

By 1850 neither doctors nor Health Boards seemed to have much idea about the cause or cure of cholera. However, a cartoon of 1849 attempted to connect the disease with the water supply, in this case the River Thames as the main source for London.

?

1 Use sources N,O, and P to describe the impact of cholera.

2 How effective were the various precautions in stopping the spread of cholera? – give reasons for your answer.

3 How effectively does the cartoon in source S show the connection between cholera and the city's drinking water?

THE WATER THAT JOHN DRINKS.

This is the water that JOHN drinks.

This is the Thames with its cento of stink,
That supplies the water that JOHN drinks.

These are the fish that float in the ink-
-y stream of the Thames with its cento of stink,
That supplies the water that JOHN drinks

This is the sewer, from cesspool and sink,
That feeds the fish that float in the ink-
-y stream of the Thames with its cento of stink,
That supplies the water that JOHN drinks.

S The water that John drinks

THE STRUGGLE TO LIVE

Between 1750 and 1850 thousands of families came to live and work in the growing towns of Britain. But, the living standards for these new town labourers could be very different.

The skilled worker could hope to live reasonably well in the towns. A brief report is given below.

Jobs	–	Mason, Joiner or Engineer
Wages	–	13s (65p) to 30s (£1.50p) per week
Wife and family	–	Lived at home – children sent to school
House	–	Flat with 2 or 3 rooms
Possessions	–	Good beds, furniture, warm clothes
Wealth	–	Small savings in the bank
Diet	–	Beef, ham, mutton, butter, cheese

However, the life of the unskilled worker was very much harder, and poverty was always present. His work in the coal mines, cotton mills or the iron works needed a lot of strength, and was often very boring.

T Weekly wages of a Glasgow labourer

1790	1812	1819	1831	1851
8s	11s	7s6d	9s	12s
(40p)	(55p)	(38p)	(45p)	(60p)

John Strang, Statistics of Glasgow, *1853*

The family income was often very low as the children earned only about 1s (5) per week, and the man was sometimes unable to find work.

U Children queue for their wages

V Single End

Most labouring families would eat, sleep and live in one room, called a 'Single End'.

In 1843 the problem of poverty in Paisley became very bad, as described by the Provost.

W I have visited a very great number of families and found many of them without a single item to sell (to the pawnbroker for money), without any furniture, without any clothes to cover themselves. Several had to borrow clothing from a neighbour to allow them to appear on the street.

Report of the Select Committee on Distress in Paisley, 1843

Life was often so miserable that many labourers spent a lot of their wages on whisky and beer. As a result, there was often very little left over for the rent and food. The labourer's family mostly ate oatmeal porridge and buttermilk, broth and potatoes, sometimes poor quality meat and fish, along with a little bread and tea. When they no longer had the strength to work, most labourers had no savings to fall back on. They were forced to beg in the streets, perhaps get some food from time to time from charity, but frequently died paupers.

?

1. Make up a chart for the unskilled labourer using the headings: Jobs, Wages, Wife and Family, House, Possessions, Wealth, and Diet. Opposite each heading, fill in a brief summary just like the chart for the skilled labourer on page 51.
2. Quote examples from both sources V and W which show the poverty of the unskilled labourer.

● *What caused poverty?*

Poverty was a common problem for almost all urban working families at some time in their lives. There were times when families were forced to live 'below the poverty line', that is they did not earn sufficient money to buy enough food, clothes or shelter.

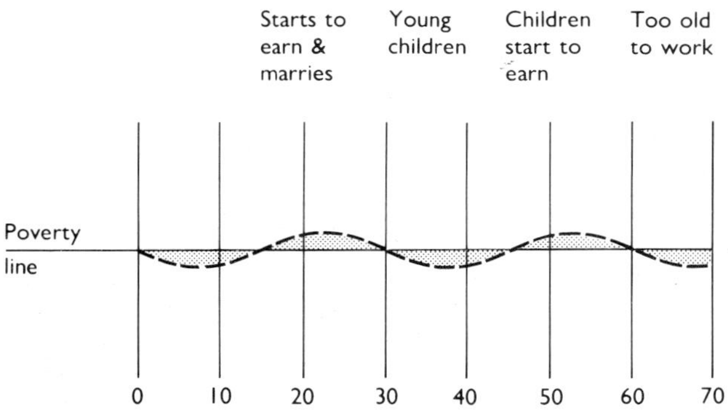

POVERTY CHART

In 1750 poor relief based on the church worked well enough in the countryside with its stable population, but this system was unable to cope with the large numbers of poor strangers who flooded into the towns from places like the Highlands or Ireland. The larger towns set up special buildings to provide shelter and food for the homeless. In Glasgow a tax on the inhabitants paid for the upkeep of 152 old men, widows and orphans in the Town's Hospital.

X The Poorhouse in Edinburgh

Licences and special badges were issued to beggars allowing them to beg in the streets of the town on specified days.

Y Beggar's Badge

How much sympathy was there really for the urban poor in Britain?

Y The poor may be persons who are able to supply their necessities by labour but are unwilling . . . they are not entitled to receive the assistance of charity. They are able to supply their own wants if they choose, and to assist them is to give a direct encouragement to idleness.

There may be persons who are of such feebleness of body or of mind as render them unable to provide for themselves . . . These are the persons whom the law chiefly contemplated in its provision for aid.

Professor McGill, Discourses and Essays on Subjects of Public Interest, *1819*

Z I have this day seen such misery. I met 20 men sweeping the street . . . they say that the introduction of machinery is the chief cause of their misery. They are now employed by the parish for 1s (5p) a day and because of the great number of paupers, they are only allowed to work two days a week. When they were employed in their own work, they could earn 5s (25p) to 7s (35p) a day and could maintain their families.

William Dodd, Letters from Leeds, *1842*

However, other ideas were also put forward for the amount of poverty. Dr Cowan from Glasgow believed that 'the labouring classes marry early, and make no provision for their children . . . each birth increasing poverty'. Dr Alison from Tranent blamed the 26 public houses in the village for the poverty there.

AA Workers in the factory

By 1843 Poor Law Commissioners were looking into the whole question of poverty in Scotland. They found many cases of genuine poverty in the towns. A mason in Greenock had been out of work for 13 months, and with his wife and three children lived in a 'bedroom stripped of every article of furniture'. His allowance for food was two pints of soup and three scones a day.

A factory worker from Aberdeen was found out of work for nine months.

BB His furniture was packed up to be taken away. He was hopeless of getting anything to relieve himself. He appeared to be a decent man: and if he had anything like constant employment, he would have been prevented from falling into the lowest class of destitute characters.

Poor Law Report, 1843

It was clear from the Commissioners' reports that there was a need to reform the old poor law. The Poor Law Amendment Act was passed in England in 1834, and its main aim was to attempt to abolish all outdoor relief payments and to force all the poor into the workhouses. The conditions in these workhouses were deliberately harsh to discourage people from seeking poor relief.

CC Living Poverty

DD Inside the Workhouse – this picture shows the grim reality of life for workhouse inmates

In 1841 half the factories in Paisley were forced to close as a result of a big slump in trade. In the next two years over 14,000 people in the town were out of work and forced to depend on poor relief. But the town's relief funds were soon exhausted, and although the crisis was relieved by private donations from the Queen and members of the Government, it showed the need for a reform of the poor law.

The Scottish Poor Law Act of 1845 tried to avoid the worst conditions of the English Act, but also wanted to reduce the money paid out to the able-bodied poor.

Results of the Poor Law Act for Scotland

1. The old and sick received outdoor relief payments.
2. Able-bodied poor without work had no right to relief payments, but had to enter poorhouses to obtain any relief.
3. Conditions in poorhouses were strict – families split up and special rules on silence, cleanliness, hours of work, and draining.
4. Money for poor relief was raised from property owners.
5. The poor law was now headed by a Board of Supervision in Edinburgh, Parochial Boards in towns and countryside, and inspectors visited the poor and poorhouses.

This Act increased the amount of money spent on the poor, from £260,000 in 1843 to £550,000 in 1848. Also, the statistics for the Town's Hospital in Glasgow show an increase in inmates from 347 in 1821 to 673 in 1847.

?

1 What were the main causes of urban poverty in Scotland?

2. Quote three pieces of evidence, along with the source or author, which show sympathy for the distress of the urban poor. In the same way, quote another three pieces of evidence which show a lack of sympathy for the poor.

3. Why was the Government forced to pass a Poor Law Act in 1845?

4. Group discussion and report. Groups are to report on the following question: Were the urban poor any better off after the Poor Law Act of 1845?

6 THE DRIVE FOR DEMOCRACY

"We want the vote"

In 1830 the ways of electing Members of Parliament had not changed for hundreds of years. They were out of date, and in need of reform.

At this time less than one person in every 50 had the right to vote. There were no women voters at all. Also, thousands of families had moved away from many country areas in Britain. Most had moved to find work in the factories in the growing towns.

The electoral system in 1830 was totally unfair.

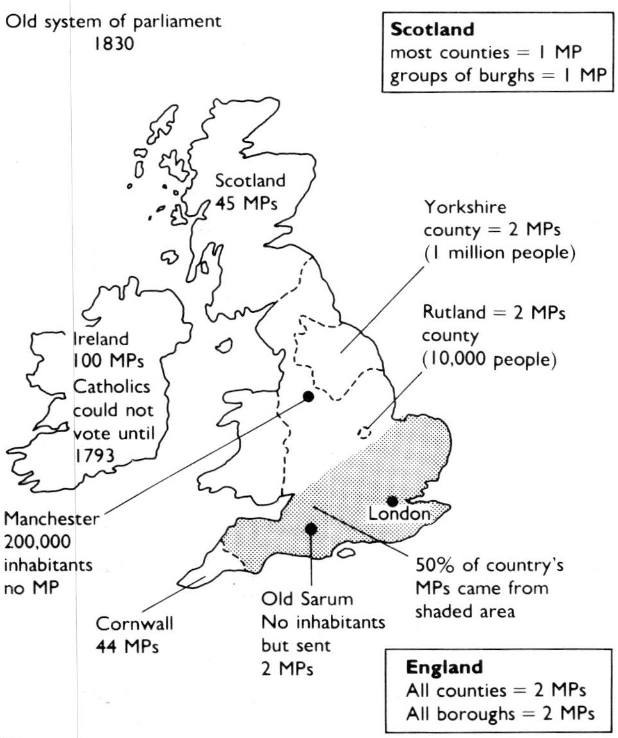

?

1 Make a list of the ways in which the old system of voting was unfair.

*V*OTING IN SCOTLAND

The Act of Union (1707) saw the end of an independent Scottish Parliament in Edinburgh. Instead, Scotland was allowed to send 45 MPs to the Parliament in London.

But, as in England, the system of electing MPs in Scotland was both unfair and corrupt, leaving thousands of people unrepresented. Voting rested with the rich and powerful in both the countryside and towns, and the ordinary working man had no say in the election of the government. Also, only royal burghs in Scotland had the right to vote, mostly in groups, for an MP. As a result, the new industrial town of Paisley with its 70,000 inhabitants had no right to an MP at all as it did not have a royal charter.

A By an Act of 1761, it was enacted that the right of voting should be in persons with property of lands of forty shillings old extent (a valuation of the thirteenth century), or £400 valued rent. By a device of the lawyers, when a person of great property wishes to multiply his votes, he appoints a number of his confidential friends to whom the Crown parcels out his estates in lots of £400 valued rent . . . and consequently all entitled to vote. (These are called fictitious voters.)

The total number of real voters in the counties is 1,390. The total number of fictitious voters is 1,201. The thirty three counties return only 30 members, six having only the right of sending a member to every second Parliament.

When the county of Caithness returns a member, he is nominated by Sir John Sinclair . . . the late Lord Melville always boasted that he could return thirty nine out of the forty five who represented the whole kingdom of Scotland.

T. H. B. Oldfield, The Representative History of Great Britain and Ireland, *1816*

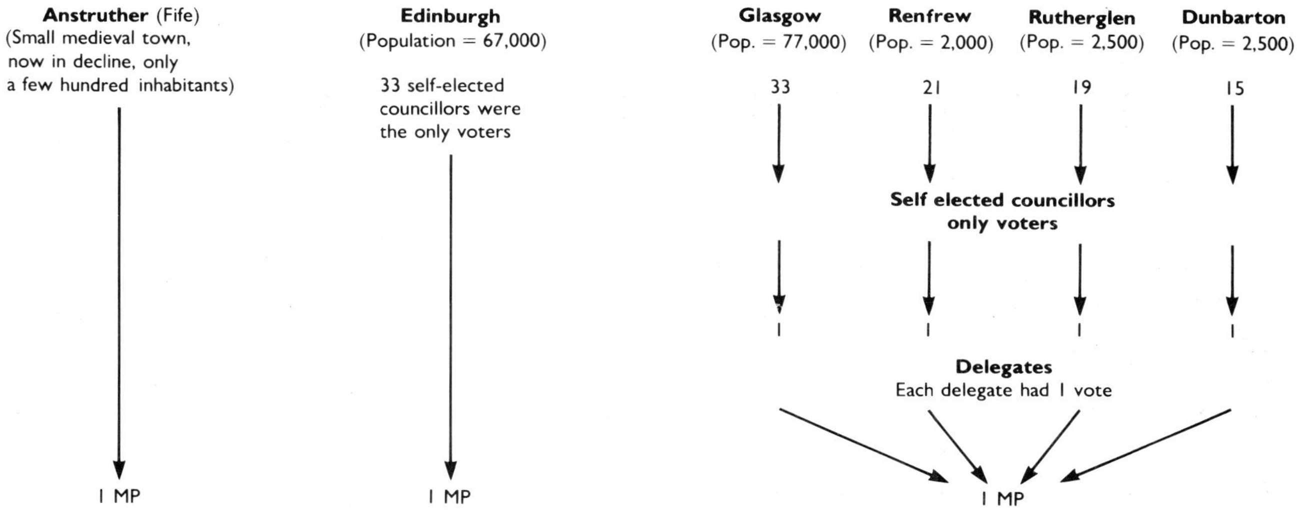

B Of fifteen members for the cities and burghs, one for Edinburgh is chosen by thirty three persons; the other fourteen by sixty five delegates, who are elected by 1,220 persons (all town councillors) . . .

The inhabitants of Scotland are above two million; their representatives are chosen by 3,844.

T. H. B. Oldfield, The Representative History of Great Britain and Ireland, *1816*

As many Parliamentary seats were controlled by powerful landowners, there were few actual elections. However, where elections did take place, there were often few voters and so bribery and corruption were very common. Further, there was no secret ballot, and a voter had to openly announce his choice to the crowd.

C Voting for an MP

D Have you ever known intimidation practiced to any extent at a county election? – Yes, by landlords over tenants.

In what ways have they exercised that intimidation? – By insisting upon their voting as the landlord wished, and it was perfectly understood by them that they would lose their farms if they voted contrary to the wishes of their landlords.

Report of the Select Committee on Bribery at Elections, 1835

E Each town-council elected a delegate; and those four or five delegates elected the member; and instead of bribing the town-councils the established practice was to bribe only the delegates or indeed only one of them.

Henry Cockburn, Memorials of his Time, *1856*

?

1 You are very unhappy about the ways of electing MPs to Parliament. Compose a letter to your local newspaper stating all the wrong features of the methods of election around 1830, and include specific examples in your letter.

2 In what ways does source C show the importance of bribery in the system of voting?

MASSACRE!

On Monday 16 August 1819, a huge crowd of about 80,000 people gathered at St Peter's Field in Manchester. They had come to hear a speech by Henry Hunt. He thought the whole system of government by Parliament should be changed, and he wanted every person to have the right to vote.

But the Government was very unhappy about the meeting of so many people in Manchester. The sources tell you what happened that day.

E Order was kept by a ban on all weapons . . . I saw a party of soldiers coming, sword in hand, round the corner . . . they dashed forward, and began cutting the people . . . their swords chopped their way through held-up hands and defenceless heads.

Samuel Bamford, Passages in the life of a Radical, *1844*

H The soldiers rode up to the meeting. At once the mob attacked them with stones and sticks, and tried to unhorse them. The soldiers charged among them, and many were hurt with sword cuts.

Letter in the Courier, *1819*

The day ended with 11 people dead and over 400 men, women and children injured.

?

1. Sources F, G and H given different views of what happened on 16 August. Decide if each source supported the crowd or the soldiers. Quote evidence from the source to support your view.
2. Prepare a newspaper front page on the Peterloo Massacre. Your page layout should include a headline, a picture and an eyewitness report.

G "Peterloo"

PROTESTS IN SCOTLAND

The success of the French people in overthrowing their king and Government in 1789 encourage radicals in Britain also to demand major reforms. Such demands were helped by the great distress felt by the labouring classes after 1815.

Causes of distress

- Disruptive effects of Agricultural and Industrial Revolutions.
- High food prices, made worse by the Corn Laws.
- Increased taxation.
- Out-of-date Poor Law system.
- Unemployment, partly due to new machinery.
- Decline of handloom weavers whose wages fell from 27s (£1.35p) a week in 1800 to 5s (25p) in the 1830s.

There was a wave of protests throughout Britain in the years after 1815, culminating with the Peterloo Massacre of 1819. The reaction of the Government was to pass the Six Acts, banning public meetings and the possession of weapons.

In the spring of 1820 the 'Radical War' broke out in Scotland. There was a general strike in Glasgow and nearby towns, and copies of the *Radical Address* were distributed all over West and Central Scotland.

People waited for the coming revolution. But in fact only a very few workers took up arms. One group led by John Baird and Andrew Hardie marched from Glasgow to the Carron Iron Works near Falkirk, only to be met there by Government troops. After a short skirmish at Bonnymuir, in which some of the marchers were killed, the leaders were arrested. Baird and Hardie were hanged while 18 others were transported to Australia for life. Another group led by James Wilson marched from Strathaven to Glasgow, but quickly dispersed on finding no support there. Wilson was also arrested and hanged.

Why did these attempted risings fail? One reason might be found in the following letter written by Capt. Mitchell, the Glasgow Police Commander, to Lord Sidmouth, the Home Secretary.

J We know that many of those involved in this treasonable plot are too weak and unorganised to carry out their wicked intent. Thus, my lord, if some plan were conceived by which the plotters could be lured out of their lairs, we could catch them undefended. The military is more than adequate to round up such vermin. I have given instructions to our informants on these lines – all good men who have infiltrated the disaffected's committees and organisation.

From Ellis and MacA'Ghobhainn, The Scottish Insurrection of 1820

ADDRESS

TO THE

Inhabitants of Great Britain & Ireland;

FRIENDS AND COUNTRYMEN,

ROUSED from that torpid state in which WE have been sunk for so many years, We are at length compelled, from the extremity of our sufferings, and the contempt heaped upon our Petitions for redress, to assert our RIGHTS, at the hazard of our lives; and proclaim to the world the real motives, which (if not misrepresented by designing men, would have United all ranks), have reduced us to take up ARMS for the redress of our *Common Grievances.*

The numerous Public Meetings held throughout the Country has demonstrated to you, that the interests of all Classes are the same. That the protection of the Life and Property of the *Rich Man,* is the interest of the *Poor Man,* and in return, it is the interest of the Rich, to protect the poor from the iron grasp of DESPOTISM; for, when its victims are exhausted in the lower circles, there is no assurance but that its ravages will be continned in the upper: For once set in motion, it will continue to move till a succession of Victims fall.

I The *Radical Address*

Reform – For or Against

One of the main demands of the radicals was the reform of Parliament. But, even with the arrival of a new Government in 1830, which was pledged to a wide programme of reforms, there was still a major debate 'for' or 'against' the reform of Parliament.

Since the old Parliamentary system worked almost completely for the benefit of the landowners, it is hardly surprising that as a class they saw no reason for changing it.

K I on my own part will go further and say that I have never read or heard of any measure to . . . satisfy my mind that the state of representation can be improved . . . I will go further and say that Parliament and the system of representation possesses the full and entire confidence of the country.

Speech by Duke of Wellington in the House of Lords, 1830 – Parliamentary Debates

The cartoon below shows what some politicians believed would happen if the vote was extended to the working people.

But, support for the reform of Parliament came mostly from the growing numbers of industrialists and working class.

M I am opposed to Universal Suffrage (the vote for all) . . . Yet, saying this, we exclude from all share in the government great masses of property and intelligence . . . We drive over to the side of revolution those whom we shut out from power.

T.B. Macaulay, Speech in the House of Commons, 1831

In 1830 Thomas Attwood formed the Birmingham Political Union to press for reform, and soon similar Unions sprang up in other towns.

N That House (of Commons), in its present state, is evidently too far removed . . . from the wants and interests of the lower and middle classes of the people . . . The great aristocratical interests of all kinds are well

L Workers in Parliament

represented there . . . But the interests of Industry and Trade have scarcely any representative at all.

Declaration of the Birmingham Political Union, 1830

?

1. What were the main reasons for the failure of the Radical revolts in Scotland in 1820?
2. Group Activity
   Make up the script of a short debate in Parliament in 1832, in which two politicians speak against the reform of Parliament and another two in favour of reform. Write the script in your own words, but use sources K, L, M and N as the basis of your information. Each member of the group could take on the role of one of the speakers. Act out the debate.

THE VOTE AT LAST

In the early 1830s there were many protests in favour of reform of Parliament. In 1832 over 10,000 people marched through the streets of Glasgow with banners saying 'Liberty or Death'.

In June 1832 the Government finally passed the Reform Act. There were separate Acts for both England and Scotland.

Results of the Scottish Reform Act

The right to vote was given to:

in towns	–	Men who owned a house or shop valued at more than £10 a year.
in the country	–	Men who owned land valued at more than £10 a year.
	–	Men who rented land valued at more than £50 a year.

Number of voters increased from 4,200 to 65,000 (population of Scotland was 2,360,000).

Voting still open (No secret ballot).

Eight more MPs given to the new industrial towns.

Each Parliament to last seven years before the next election.

?

1. Would the following have the vote after the 1832 Reform Act?

A. Laird with a landed estate worth £4,000 a year.

B. Cotton worker with a small single room at a rent of £4 a year?

C. Woman who owned land valued at £100 a year?

D. Shopkeeper with a store worth £200 a year?

E. Farmer who rented his land for £100 a year?

F. Farm labourer who rented a croft for £10 a year?

2. Was the Scottish Reform Act a success or a failure? In your group discussion on this question, you should write down at least three points you could include under success and also under failure.

REACTION TO THE REFORM

On 7 June 1832 Parliament was reformed for the first time in several hundred years. But how great were the changes in fact?

Certainly the right to vote in both the countryside and the towns of Britain was increased from 435,000 to 652,000, yet still five out of six men were left without the vote. The transfer of Parliamentary seats from depopulated constituencies to the new industrial towns gave merchants and factory owners access to Parliament, and it also gave a similar opportunity to some Radicals like William Cobbett who was elected MP for Oldham.

However, Parliament did not change a great deal after 1832, the landowning class was still in control. The real importance of the Reform Act was more that it was the first stage in the process towards a truly democratic Parliament.

Reactions to the 1832 Reform Act varied from one section of society to another.

The Whig party under Earl Grey had put forward the Reform Bill, and hoped that the new middle-class town voters would vote solidly for them. The Whigs only contemplated a moderate reform of Parliament.

O After 1832 the middle classes remained reluctant to [take part] in protest. They also [kept] all their determination not to allow the workers a greater influence in politics. The reforms might be a disappointment, but it was better than plunging towards democracy.

To the Whigs, the Act was a success in that the existing order was preserved.

Michael Brock, The Great Reform Act, *1973*

The Tory party under the Duke of Wellington was opposed to any changes in the Parliamentary system.

P I don't think the influence of property in this country is diminished. That is to say that the landowners have as many followers, and influence as many voters at elections as ever they did.

Duke of Wellington, The Croker Papers, *1884*

The Radicals had hoped for a major reform of Parliament which would allow working men to vote and also become MPs.

Q It was the fond wish of the people that a remedy for their grievances would be found in the Reform Act of 1832. They have been bitterly deceived . . . The Reform Act has brought about the transfer of power from one controlling group to another, and left the people helpless as before.

The Chartist Petition, 1838

?

1 Use sources O, P and Q to explain the following statement about the Reform Act.
The Whigs (Merchant class) were satisfied.
The Tories (Landowning class) were relieved.
The Radicals (Working class) were angry.

THE CHARTISTS

In the 1830s life for most working people was very harsh and unpleasant. Many people believed that the only way to improve matters was to get working people elected by Parliament. But the 1832 Reform Act had not made that possible, and working people were left angry and disappointed.

In 1836 William Lovett of the London Working Men's Association drew up a list of demands. The aim was to give the ordinary working man a much greater say in Parliament.

It was called The People's Charter.

The Six Points of the People's Charter

1. **A vote** for every man 21 years of age, of sound mind, and not in prison.
2. The **ballot**, to protect the voter.
3. **No property qualification** for MPs, to allow poor men to stand for Parliament.
4. **Payment of MPs**, to allow working men to give up their jobs to stand for Parliament.
5. **Equal constituencies**, same number of voters in each constituency.
6. **Annual Parliaments**, to make it more difficult for voters to be bribed.

The people who supported these new demands were called Chartists. They now began to gather a huge petition which would be presented to the Government along with the Charter. They hoped that if enough people signed the petition, the Government would agree to their demands. At the same time, large demonstrations were organised. On 21 May 1838 over 200,000 people turned up to a Chartist meeting on Glasgow Green.

The first Chartist Petition with 1,300,000 signatures was presented to the Government in 1839. It was rejected. In the following years, thousands of people in England and Scotland joined the Chartists. By 1840 there were over 100 Chartist Branches in Scotland.

During the 1840s the Chartists used various methods to persuade the Government to give workers the vote. There were meetings held all over the country, while Chartist newspapers like The *Northern Star* and The *True Scotsman* were read widely. Other petitions were organised, in 1842 3,000,000 people signed it, and by 1848 there were 6,000,000 names, but over half were false.

The Chartists also set up their own schools and churches for the factory workers. They started up their own co-operative stores which sold good food at prices the workers could afford.

R A Chartist Meeting

S Chartist Store at Hawick, 1839

It became clear that the Government was not going to give in to the Chartists. Riots and strikes became more common. The Government was afraid of revolution, and used the police and army to restore order.

T An ugly crowd collected on Glasgow Green, claiming that they were starving, and marched through the main streets of the city, entering and looting shops as they went.
The soldiers were called in . . . and were forced to fire into the crowd, killing six and wounding several others. Sixty-four people were arrested after the riots.

Glasgow Herald, *16 March 1848*

After 1848 the Chartist movement began to collapse.

?

1. Make up an imaginative poster supporting the Chartist cause.
2. Class Discussion. How many of the Six Points in the Charter are part of our Parliamentary system today?
3. Make a list of the methods used by the Chartists in their campaign against the Government.
4. Was the writer of source T for or against the Chartists? Quote evidence from the source to support your opinion.

RISE AND FALL OF CHARTISM

Chartism attracted a great deal of support from the working people of Scotland. Steady support came from the miners of Lanarkshire and the cotton spinners of Glasgow, but more active backing came from the thousands of handloom weavers whose lives had been made a misery by low wages and unemployment.

Many Chartists believed that their claims were reasonable, and that a reformed Parliament with working-class MPs would carry out changes that would improve the lives of the ordinary people. They tried to persuade the Government to listen to their views, and as a consequence gradual change would result. Supporters of this approach were called Moral Force Chartists, led by William Lovett and men like Revd Patrick Brewster of Paisley.

U Muskets are not what are wanted, but education and schooling of the working people . . . Violent works do not slay the enemies but the friends of the movement. O'Connor wants to take everything by storm, and to pass the Charter into law within a year. All this hurry and haste, this bluster and menace of armed opposition can only lead to . . . the destruction of Chartism.

Life and Struggle of William Lovett, *1876*

But some Chartists believed that the Government could not be moved into reform by words alone, and that a degree of violence was needed to force the Government into change. The Physical Force Chartists were led by men like Feargus O'Connor and John Taylor of Irvine ('Radical Jack') and they soon became involved in riots and strikes.

V Shall it be said, fellow countrymen, that four millions of men, capable of bearing arms, and defending their country against every foreign attacker, allowed a few domestic oppressors to enslave and degrade them? . . . We have resolved to obtain our rights 'peacably if we may, forcibly if we must;' but woe to those who begin the warfare with the millions, or who forcibly resist their peaceful agitation for justice.

True Scotsman, 1839

W A Physical Force Chartist arming for a fight.

The chartist campaign

1836 William Lovett founded the London Working Men's Association. Their demands were contained in The People's Charter.

1838 Large meetings in several British cities in support of Charter.

1839 Chartist Convention (Parliament) met in London. First Petition with 1,300,000 signatures presented to Parliament – rejected. Chartists under John Frost tried to take over Newport – clashed with Government troops. About 20 people killed.
'Sacred Month' – A general strike called for a month proposed, but it received little support.

1840 Most Chartist leaders, including O'Connor and Lovett, arrested.

1842 Second Petition with 3,000,000 signatures presented to Parliament – again rejected. 'Plug Plots' – A wave of strikes, but hunger forced most of the strikers back to work.

1845 Chartist Land Company set up by O'Connor. It bought land and workers could get small plots by buying shares in the Company. O'Connor knew little about land or finance, and the Company ended in a financial mess in 1852.

1848 Third Petition presented to Parliament. It became a public joke as over half of the 6,000,000 signatures were forged, with names like 'Queen Victoria' and 'Flat Nose'. It was also rejected.

By 1848 the Chartist movement was failing. O'Connor had hoped for a crowd of 500,000 to attend a rally on Kennington Common in London, but in fact only about 20,000 turned up. Also the Government was so frightened of violence that it recruited hundreds of armed constables to protect the city.

At the same time trade had begun to improve, leading to more jobs and higher wages. The coming of prosperity encouraged many workers to turn their attention away from Chartism.

X Newport Rising, 1839

?

1 In your own words, describe the aims of the Moral and Physical Force Chartists from sources U and V.

2 In what different ways is the cartoonist in source W trying to make fun of the Physical Force Chartists?

3 Group Work. In groups, make a list of the reasons for the failure of the Chartist campaign.

7 THE CHURCH IN CHARGE

During the eighteenth century most people belonged to the Presbyterian Church of Scotland. There were some Episcopalians in Aberdeenshire, while the Roman Catholic faith was still strong in the North West. The Church of Scotland was divided into parishes, and the Minister of each parish church held a strong control over the lives and welfare of the ordinary people in his parish. In this work, he was helped by elders, the members of the Kirk Session. The ministers themselves were mostly appointed by the local landowners.

The ministers and Kirk Session had a lot of power in the parish.
They:

- looked after the poor of the parish.
- looked after education in the parish school.
- looked after baptism, marriages and funerals.
- looked after the morals and behaviour of the people of the parish.

The elders were very strict about behaviour. They patrolled the streets looking for sin, and made frequent visits to family homes. People who were found drunk or swearing, or even those who had not attended church every Sunday without good reason, came to the attention of the elders. Such people were either fined, or else forced to stand before the entire church on the Stool of Repentance, while they were severely told off by the minister.

A The Stool of Repentance

B A.G. and J.R. were found guilty of bad behaviour in laughing and throwing stones in church, and of cutting and eating apples in church: to appear four times before the kirk session meeting and pay 40 shillings (£2).

Gordon, Chronicles of Keith, *1723*

Religion played a very important part in family life in the eighteenth century. The father would take a short service every morning and evening. Regular readings from the family bible were common. The children had further instruction from the bible in the parish schools.

On Sunday, or the Sabbath as it was called, all work and recreation was forbidden. The whole family had to attend the parish church. The service was held in very plain surroundings, with no music at all. The main part of the service was the sermon, when the minister would talk at the congregation for around two hours.

This is what the family of merchant George Brown did each Sunday.

C Rose at 7 in the morning, prayed then joined in family worship, and then read from the bible. Went to the North West Church and heard Mr. M'Laurin preach. Went to Church in the afternoon; heard sermon on the same text as the morning. Returned and joined in family worship: supped and retired; thought about the sermon again and wrote down the main headings of it.

Diary of George Brown, *merchant, 1745-53*

But, from around 1800, the power and influence of the church in Scotland began to decline. Thousands of families were to move away from the strong control of the country minister and Kirk Session to live in the growing cities. There were fewer churches in the poorer parts of the towns, and often factory workers were too tired to go regularly to church.

The rigid discipline of the Church of Scotland also relaxed in the cities. More moderate ministers allowed the members much greater freedom to enjoy themselves.

?

1. Class discussion
   The class should discuss how a typical Sunday in the eighteenth century is different from a Sunday today.
2. Role playing
   Groups in the class should write a script for a play on a family Sunday in a country parish. The family should be made up of a father, mother and three children. The script should include what the family did throughout the Sunday, with a special part on what happened during the church services.
   The best script should be acted out, with that group taking the parts of the family, and the rest of the class forming the church congregation.

THE KIRK, THE POOR AND THE SCHOOL

The church accepted that it had a duty to provide for the poor of the parish. Sir John Sinclair described the role of the elder of the Kirk Session as follows: he should

- acquaint himself with the character and condition of the poor.
- keep an accurate list of the poor in the parish.
- make frequent visits to the poor in their houses.
- watch over the moral and religious interests of the poor.
- receive and distribute funds for the relief of the poor.

The funds for poor relief came from a variety of sources, but mostly from weekly church collections, fines imposed for non-attendance at church and other offences, or private donations.

However, a falling standard of living and growing unemployment in the countryside caused an increase in the numbers of poor in rural parishes. This put considerable strain on parish charity and made it necessary to introduce Assessments, a form of tax on all landholders. By 1800, 92 out of a total of 878 parishes in Scotland had introduced a system of Assessments to raise more money for poor relief, and the number had increased to 230 by 1845.

The success of the parish Kirk Session in providing for the needs of its poor varied greatly throughout the country.

D The number of poor who are on the pension list and receive weekly alms from the Kirk Session is eighty. They can only receive from 6d (2½p) to 1s (5) each, which, although it may assist them a little, is by no means able to support them in their own houses. Begging, therefore, is allowed and is a great burden on the inhabitants. The poor will never be suitably provided for until the owners of land agree to assess themselves in a sum that may be adequate to this purpose.

Old Statistical Account, Parish of Kilmarnock, 1792

E The regular provision for the poor of this parish is very liberal. The family of the Duke of Hamilton give very handsome donations. About the year 1750, the inhabitants, in order to put a stop to begging, and to give more regular relief to the modest poor, assessed themselves in the payment of annual poor's rates, the amount of which was then about £100. With this and the other funds, all the poor (then upwards of fifty) were decently supported and begging was strictly prohibited. Claimants for public charity, however, becoming more numerous, the list was increased to 115 and the annual rates to £230.

There are also ten charitable institutions, formed by people of different occupations for the relief of any of their members who may fall into distress. The most important of these are the weavers, who give to each of their members, while on a bed of sickness, 3s (15p) weekly, and when in a state of recovery but unable to work 2s (10p). The number of beggars, belonging to this parish, is small compared to the crowds of vagrants who spread over the country, begging, cheating, or stealing.

Old Statistical Account, Parish of Hamilton, 1729

Education

In the eighteenth century, control over the parish schools in the country was held by the local minister and landowner. Attendance at school was not compulsory, and although teaching had to be paid for in most cases, many parents were anxious to provide an education for their children. However, the quality of education varied considerably from one parish to another.

F There is a school house, and a very good schoolmaster. His salary is paid by the landowners; which with the school fees, may amount to £18 to £20 a year; a poor pittance to live on for a man of education . . . The number of scholars may be from 50 to 60. They are taught reading English, writing, arithmetic, geometry, accounts, and a few even Latin.

Old Statistical Account, Parish of Dornock in Dumfries, 1792

G The parish school

H The average number of scholars is 10. The smallness of the number is owing to the age and infirmity of the teacher, who is above 70 years of age; to his ignorance of the languages, and to his want of a school-house. He has only a small cottage, and an area of about 8 feet by 16, taken off at the end of it as his school; and even this is crammed with tables, forms, and other household stuff. The fees for teaching to read English is 1s (5p), writing and arithmetic 1s 6d (7½p) the quarter.

Old Statistical Account, Parish of Heriot in Midlothian, 1792

I The numbers educated at the parish school may be from sixty to eighty. School fees are paid weekly, which is a bar to the regular attendance of the children.

Old Statistical Account, Parish of Tranent in East Lothian, 1799

J The scholars pay only for the time of their attendance and there is a vacation of six weeks during the harvest. The children of day labourers are often taken from school to herd cattle through the summer, attending the school only in the winter. The Kirk Sessions pay for the children of the poor, from the Poors' Funds, in teaching them to read. The schoolmaster, when there is a demand for it, teaches a night school by candle light . . . where those who had received less education in their youth attended for writing and arithmetic.

Old Statistical Account, Parish of Newlands in Peebles, 1799

?

1 Quote evidence directly from sources D and E which shows how badly the system of poor relief was organised in the parish of Kilmarnock, and how well it was run in the parish of Hamilton.

2 You have been sent to inspect the quality of schooling in Scotland at the end of the eighteenth century. Your written report should make use of information from sources F to J under the following headings: teachers: finance: accommodation: pupils: curriculum: attendance.

8 THE NEW TOWN

By 1760 the rich people of Edinburgh were no longer content to live in the noisy, smelly, overcrowded tenements of the Old Town. Provost George Drummond believed that a New Town could be built on the open land to the North of Edinburgh. A start was made by draining the Nor' Loch and building the North Bridge to join the old and new towns. In 1767 the Town Council set up a competition for the best plan for the New Town, and it was won by a young architect called James Craig. His plan was for rows of wide, straight streets and open squares.

James Craig's plan for the New Town of Edinburgh took 40 years to build, and it resulted in one of the most famous planned towns in Europe. The houses were very elegant, and contained several rooms for the families and servants of the lawyers, doctors and merchants of Edinburgh.

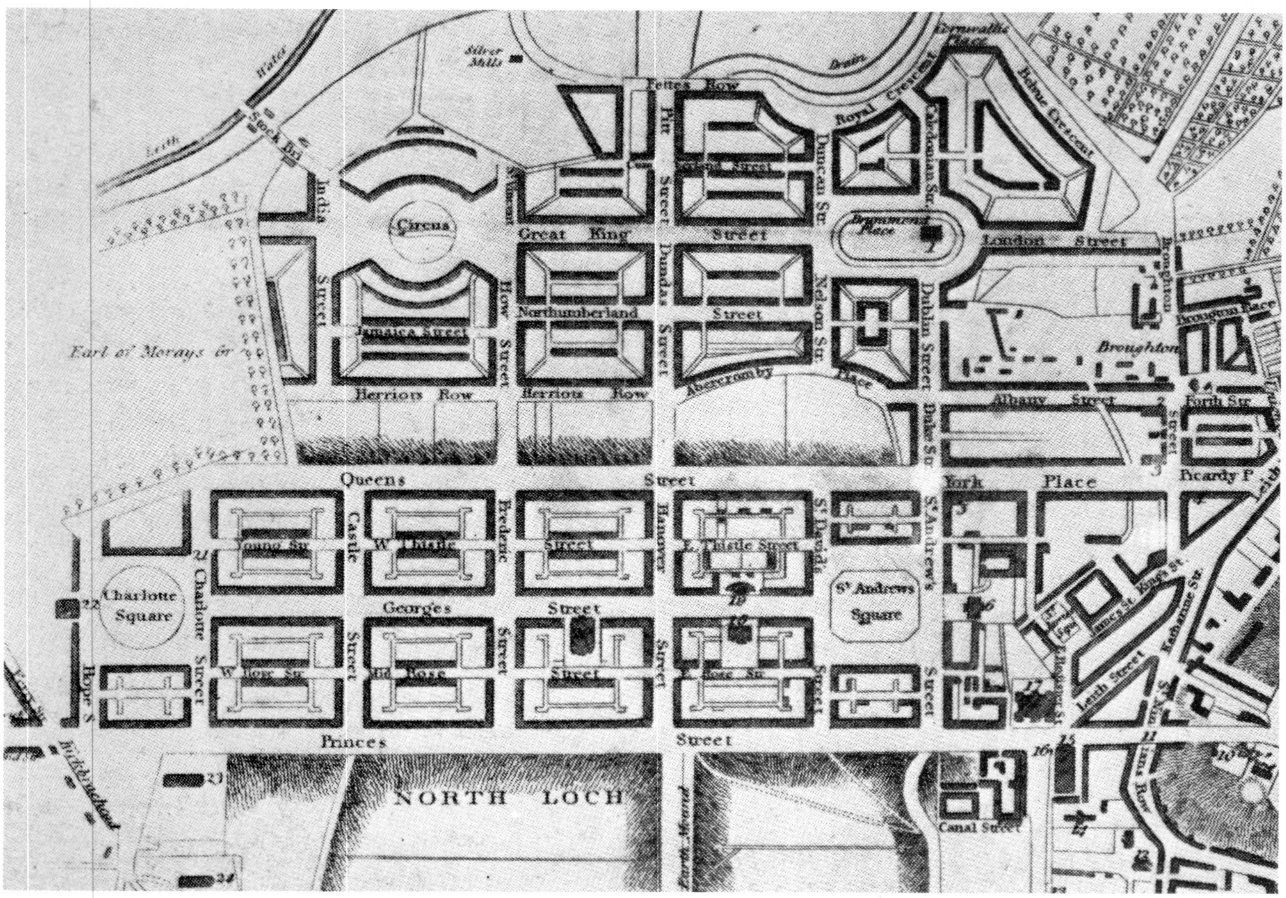

A Plan of the New Town

B St Andrew's Square

Most people who came to Edinburgh believed that the New Town was a much more pleasant place to live compared to the Old Town. But not all visitors agreed with this view.

C The view from the New Town is as beautiful as almost any country can afford. There is a supply of excellent water; and in the neighbourhood, there is a good supply of stone quarries, firstly for building houses and lastly for paving the streets.

Hugo Arnot, The History of Edinburgh, *1788*

D In designing the New Town we were led into a blunder of long straight lines of street, divided to the inch into rectangular shapes, every house being exactly the same as its neighbour, with no sign of ornaments which might vary the appearance.

Lord Cockburn, Memorials of His Time, *1807*

?

1. Imagine that you are a lawyer employed by a rich Edinburgh merchant, who is thinking about moving from the Old Town to the New Town. You have visited the New Town, and have now to write a letter to the merchant stating why you think it would be a more pleasant place for him to live in.
2. Which writer was in favour, and which one was against, the New Town? Give two reasons for each writer's point of view.

CULTURE IS HERE

From the middle of the eighteenth century Scotland was fast becoming an important centre of art and culture in Western Europe. This was the start of the age of the Scottish Enlightenment, which was to last for over 60 years.

Edinburgh, in particular, was to gain a reputation for encouragement of learning and knowledge, even overtaking the cities of London and Paris, and as a result was given the title of 'The Athens of the North'. Distinguished scholars, as well as the sons of noblemen, prevented from visiting the Continent on the Grand Tour by the lengthy wars with France, came to spend time in discussion with the famous artists, writers and philosophers of Edinburgh. Many such meetings and exchanges of ideas were conducted in the numerous clubs and societies of the city.

The meeting of so many scholars produced a flood of intellectual publications: in 1771 the first edition of the *Encyclopedia Britannica* was published in Edinburgh, while in 1802 the *Edinburgh Review* magazine gave intellectuals the opportunity to introduce new ideas on all aspects of literature and society. Edinburgh also became the centre of literary activity. During the next 80 years Scotland produced a host of famous poets, novelists, historians, economists and philosophers, far too numerous to mention individually here.

It was fashionable to have an interest in art. Rich gentlemen paid a lot of money to send artists to Greece and Italy, either to learn to paint in the Classical style or to collect antique statues and vases. Many artists were left to die in poverty but others, like David Wilkie, were able to live comfortably on their painting reputation. Wilkie's painting of a *Penny Wedding*, which showed a simple scene from ordinary Scottish life, was for the Prince Regent, but was later engraved and the prints sold widely throughout the country.

E Public exhibition of paintings, 1761

F Inside a country house

It was also the custom among the rich to have family portraits painted by artists like Henry Raeburn. There was plenty of work for famous architects like Robert Adam, who not only designed many of the buildings in the New Town of Edinburgh in the style of Greece or Rome, but also the fireplaces, furniture and carpets of the rooms in the new houses.

● *Robert Burns – a particular example*

On 25 January 1759 Robert Burns was born in Alloway near Ayr into a family of tenant farmers. Because of his father's ill health he was forced to work on the family farm, but his education was not neglected. Robert and his brother were taught at the local school in Dalrymple by a young schoolmaster called John Murdoch.

A legal dispute with the landlord and the death of his father forced Robert and his brother Gilbert to sell the farm at Lochlea and rent a smaller one at Mossgiel near Mauchline. The brothers had little money to invest in the farm and because it was on high ground it was very difficult to get a good harvest. The failure of the Mossgiel farm made Robert very bitter and he contemplated emigrating to Jamaica.

Despite his problems, Burns found comfort in writing poems and songs, some about his girlfriends Jean Armour and Mary Campbell. Although his letters revealed that he could write well in English, he found his native Scots dialect a much more expressive language for his poetry.

In a desperate effort to raise money in 1786, he persuaded a Kilmarnock printer to publish the handwritten copies of his poems. The Kilmarnock Edition of *Poems, Chiefly in the Scottish Dialect* contained most of Burn's poetry, and the entire stock of 612 copies at 3 shillings (15p) each was sold within a month.

G The Kilmarnock Edition

Much of Burn's personal resentment can be seen in his poetry, as in *The Twa Dogs* where he criticises the comfortable life of the landlords.

H "Our laird gets in his racked(1) rents,
His coal, his kane(2), an' a' his stents.(3)
He rises when he likes himsel;
His flunkies(4) answer at the bell;
He ca's his coach, he ca's his horse;
He draws a bonny silken purse,
As lang's my tail, where, through the steeks(5)
The yellow-lettered Geordie(6) keeks.'
" 'A cottar howkin(7) in a sheugh,(8)
Wi' dirty stanes biggin a dyke,
Barin' a quarry, an' sic like,
Himself, a wife he thus sustains,
A smytrie(9) o' wee duddy weans, (10)
An' nought but his han'darg(11) to keep
Them right and tight in thack(12) and
rape." (13)

Robert Burns, The Twa Dogs, *1786*

Glossary
1 = extortionate
2 = food rent
3 = another type of rent
4 = servants
5 = stitches
6 = valuable coin
7 = digging
8 = ditch
9 = collection
10 = ragged children
11 = work by hand
12 = house
13 = food

Burns became famous overnight, and when a second edition of his poems was published in Edinburgh a year later, he was invited to the houses of rich and noble families in the capital.

I Poem recital at the Duchess of Gordon's party

Burns became a national figure in Edinburgh in the winter of 1786-7, and the novelist Henry MacKenzie referred to him as 'this heaven-taught ploughman'. Burns returned to Ayrshire as a farmer at Ellisland, and then as an exciseman at Dumfries. During this time he continued to pour out verses of all descriptions, especially songs based on old Scottish folk songs. He then wrote one of his most famous poems *Tam o' Shanter*, the story of Tam's ride home after a night's drinking in a tavern. He continued to tour Scotland from the Highlands to the Borders reciting his poems and songs.

Despite the fame his works attracted throughout the length of the country, Burns did not receive the fortune he perhaps deserved. The reasons are many; maybe he insulted too many important people in the church and upper classes or maybe he spent too much time in taverns and with women. His last few years were a continual struggle against illness and poverty. He was only 36-years-old when he died in 1796.

?

1. What evidence is there in sources E and F, and in the text, that art and architecture were very popular in Scotland?
2. Write a critical report on how Burns exposed the injustice in Scottish society in source G. You should include quotations from the source in your report.

SCOTLAND 1850

By 1850 thousands of families in Scotland had moved from the countryside to the towns. But life in these new industrial towns was still a mixture of luxury and poverty.

A

B

C

D

Discuss and prepare a report for the rest of the class based on the evidence in sources A to D. The report should describe the industrialist's life of luxury and the worker's life of poverty.

INDEX